Electricity for the Entertainment Electrician & Technician

Electricity for
the Entertainment
Electrician & Technician

Richard Cadena

ELSEVIER

AMSTERDAM • BOSTON • HEIDELBERG • LONDON • NEW YORK
OXFORD • PARIS • SAN DIEGO • SAN FRANCISCO
SINGAPORE • SYDNEY • TOKYO

Focal Press is an imprint of Elsevier

Focal Press is an imprint of Elsevier
30 Corporate Drive, Suite 400, Burlington, MA 01803, USA
Linacre House, Jordan Hill, Oxford OX2 8DP, UK

Library of Congress Cataloging-in-Publication Data
Cadena, Richard.
    Electricity for the entertainment electrician & technician / Richard Cadena.
        p. cm.
    Includes bibliographical references and index.
    ISBN 978-0-240-80995-3 (pbk. : alk. paper) 1. Electricity–Safety
measures. 2. Electric circuits. 3. Electric wiring, Indoor. 4. Stage
lighting. 5. Leisure industry–Electric equipment. I. Title.
    TK152.C2185 2009
    621.319'24–dc22

                                 2008046915

British Library Cataloguing-in-Publication Data
A catalogue record for this book is available from the British Library.

ISBN: 978-0-240-80995-3

For information on all Focal Press publications
visit our website at www.books.elsevier.com

11   5 4 3

Printed in the United States of America

This book is dedicated to the most dedicated people I know — Yolanda and Noe Cadena, a.k.a., Mom and Dad.

Contents

Contents

ix

Contents

Preface

There's an ancient story of a martial arts master who attempts to give one of his students, the "chosen one," the secret to harnessing the power of the universe. But the two of them discover that the sacred scroll containing the secret is nothing but a blank reflective surface. Eventually, the student realizes the true meaning of the scroll, that the power of the universe is already inside of him. Armed with this newfound knowledge, the student becomes the master and defeats the evil warrior.

You may recognize this ancient story as the plot of the movie *Kung Fu Panda*. Yes, I realize that it's a children's animated movie about a noodle-making panda bear with no formal martial arts training who is chosen over five highly skilled experts to fulfill a prophecy by defeating the villain. And I do realize that the movie is designed to appeal more to the funny bone than to the think muscle. But as I was in the process of writing the final chapter of this book, I took my 11-year-old daughter to see this movie. I couldn't help thinking that its message, that the greatest power is inside of us all, is exactly the message that I want to convey to you, the reader, about this book. The "sacred scroll" that you now hold in your hands is nothing more than a highly reflective surface. It merely reflects the incredible power of your mind to visualize, analyze, and comprehend. That power is inside of you, and my hope is that this book will help you bring it out.

But before you undertake the journey through these pages, take some time to reflect on what it might take to reach your goals. How much effort are you willing to put forth? How much time can you spend each day working to achieve your desires? Someone once said that if you're interested in something you'll do what's convenient, but if you're passionate about something you'll do whatever it takes. No student has ever mastered a subject without making great sacrifices. It takes time, dedication, hard work, contemplation, and concerted effort. It's no

different whether we're talking about the martial arts, theatre arts, performing arts, or the art of mastering electricity.

The information contained in this book is not difficult, but it can be challenging. Some of the concepts can challenge your ability to straddle the line between abstract thought and real-world application. But if you love the production arts as much as Po, the kung fu panda, loves food and the martial arts, then you too are capable of impressive feats of artistry. All it takes now is for you to see your reflection in these pages. So I challenge you to dive into this book with the same enthusiasm as a panda bear fighting for a dumpling.

Namaste.

Acknowledgments

If I were to acknowledge everyone who truly deserves credit for helping me complete this book, the musical conductor would start playing the music long before I was finished reading my list. But there are a few key people who need to be acknowledged before they drag me from the stage with the big hook. Among them are the people who incubated the idea for this book, including John Huntington, Associate Professor of Entertainment Technology at New York City College of Technology, and Cara Anderson, Acquisitions Editor at Focal Press. Also, Valerie Geary, Associate Acquisitions Editor, Danielle Monroe, Associate Acquisitions Editor (yes, it's *finally* done!), and all the wonderful people at Focal Press deserve special thanks for their hard work and exceptionally positive attitude.

And then there are a few people who were gracious enough to answer a barrage of questions and never once complained. In alphabetical order, they are: Tony Giovannetti, The Metropolitan Opera; Mitch Hefter, Entertainment Technology; Dave Isherwood, White Light, Ltd.; François Juliat, Robert Juliat; Fred Mikeska, AC Lighting; E. H. B. "Chipmonck" Monck; Daniele Peroni, Link S.R.L.; Bill Plachy, I.A.T.S.E. Local 1; M. Eric Rimes, Lighting Faculty at North Carolina School of the Arts; Bob See, See Factor Lighting; Steve Terry, ETC; Ken Vannice, Leviton; Richard Wolpert, Union Connector; and Mike Wood, Mike Wood Consulting.

And, of course, there are two very special people who give meaning to my life and work, and they are my beautiful wife and daughter, Lisa and Joanna "Joey" Cadena. Thank you for being there for me.

There are many, many more people who, in one way or another, helped make this book possible. So let me say thank you to one and all, and I'm going to get off the stage now before I get booted off. [*Standby fade to black … and go!*]

WHAT IS AN ENTERTAINMENT ELECTRICIAN*?

In the theatre, the director directs, the actors act, the designers design, the riggers rig, and the flyman flies. But electricians, by some twist of logic, are responsible for an array of technology, including supplying electricity in a safe and efficient manner. They are also responsible for making sure that everything that is connected to show power is properly rigged, configured, and functioning. The same applies to the production electricians or entertainment electricians who work in a variety of fields — concert tours, industrial and corporate events, theme parks, cruise ships, and more.

A good master electrician needs to have an excellent grasp not only of electricity (no, not literally!), but also of electronics, networking, rigging, safety, local codes and regulations, and everything else involved with keeping the show up and running from a standpoint of safety first and operation second. What, then, is an electrician in the entertainment industry? What distinguishes an electrician from a technician? The answer is not always clear cut, and it might vary from venue to venue, from region to region, and from job to job. But on the most basic level, an electrician is typically responsible for making sure that show power is available for every device that requires it in order to make the show a success. In some instances that means that he or she must "tie in" the feeder cable to the main supply, or in the case of a theatre or other venue where power is already distributed to the stage electrics, make

*In the province of Quebec, Canada, a person is not legally an electrician unless they are licensed as such. Therefore, the person who does the job that would be called a master electrician, production electrician, or an entertainment technician is referred to as a "technician."

sure it is distributed properly. But that's not where the electrician's area of responsibility ends.

Almost all of the responsibility for making sure all of the gear plays well together rests on the backs of the electricians and technicians. That increasingly means rigging a device and running power to it, using the right hardware to make the connection, knowing how networks are wired and distributed, configuring computerized devices like automated lighting and media servers, and more.

The show must go on, but it must go on safely. And the electrician must do his or her part to make sure there are no technological glitches.

TECHNOLOGY MOVES ON

In a field where lighting, audio, and video rigs are becoming larger and more complex, the electricians and technicians are shouldering more and more responsibility for a diverse range of equipment. Add to that the fast pace of change in technology, and it becomes clear just how challenging it can be to stay on top of the situation.

While many shows are raising production values to meet the demand of the discriminating public, budgets are getting tighter, accountants are exercising more control, and greater scrutiny is being placed on cash flow. As a result, larger and more efficient rigs are being managed by smaller crews, which means that show personnel are given more responsibility and fewer human resources with which to work. When the Hilary Duff tour hit the road a few years ago, they were carrying a medium-sized rig with several automated lights, conventionals, a laser system, and video for image magnification (I-mag). But they had only two lighting crew and two video crew. The bulk of the manual labor was handled by local crew hired for the day, but the responsibility for making sure it all worked remained with the touring crew. One of the lighting crew took care of the front of house while the other took responsibility for everything else. You can be sure they both knew everything there was to know about the rig to keep it going.

In the early 1900s, theatres on Broadway were among the first customers of the Edison Electric Illuminating Company. The DC generators and

distribution systems remained in operation there for decades. Originally, theatre owners resisted converting to AC power because there was no incentive to spend the money it required. That meant that electricians were primarily concerned with luminaires and dimmers; there were no consoles, no electronics, no computers, and no need to understand any of this technology in the theatre. Eventually, some theatre owners acquiesced and converted to AC power. In the process, they discovered that the labor-saving dimmers paid for themselves, and soon, all the other theatres on Broadway followed suit. Suddenly, the job description of the master electrician had changed forever, bringing with it new responsibilities. Not only did the lighting and dimmers have to be hung, connected, and working, but the console at the front of house also had to be dealt with. Many of the oldtimers couldn't change with the times and lost their jobs. Those who were adaptable and willing to learn new technology thrived.

Soon after the computerized console came the first automated lighting systems, the first DMX-controlled media servers, and the first digital lighting systems. Now the master electrician, show electrician, production electrician, or lighting technician, whose first responsibility is to make sure a show is hung and working properly, is dealing with an array of new technology.

KEEPING UP WITH TECHNOLOGY

Change is a way of life, and today technology is moving at a faster pace than ever before. Building a career as a professional in the entertainment industry requires a solid grasp of the technology we use on a daily basis. In order to be a competent electrician or technician, you have to keep up with a variety of technologies and practices, which may seem like a monumental task. At times it can be a bit overwhelming. But no matter how much technology changes, the basic principles are still the same. Just as the law of gravity remains constant over time, so does Ohm's law and dozens of other laws of nature that dictate the behaviors of all things technological. If you understand these fundamentals and apply them to current technology, it will take much less effort to stay on top of this changing industry.

I once taught a seminar on automated lighting to a group of lighting techs. On the last day of the three-day seminar, one of the techs who had been sitting in the back of the room all three days spoke up.

"I don't really need to know this stuff," he said. "I'm perfectly happy working on conventional lights."

"Then why are you here?" I asked.

"Because my boss sent me," came the reply.

"But your company owns a lot of automated lights. What do you do when they need service?" I asked.

"I let the young guys work on them."

Not long after the seminar, a group of terrorists flew two planes into the World Trade Center and one into the Pentagon. The Lighting Dimensions International (LDI) trade show in Orlando held soon thereafter was sparsely attended, and the industry reeled from the economic fallout. I don't know what became of that tech, but I often wonder how he fared in the ensuing downturn in the industry. I also wonder if he had children, and if so, if he would advise them to learn about new technology or shun it. And I wonder if he ever used what he learned in that class. I'm betting he did.

OVERVIEW

Over the last few years, I've been leading seminars on electricity for the entertainment electrician and technician. In one of the more recent events there were several very experienced electricians in attendance. During the course of the seminar, a question came up about a formula I was using, and another formula was tossed out by one of the attendees. I struggled to reconcile the two formulas. Eventually, I convinced myself that the original formula was correct, but I failed to convince most of the class.

After the seminar was over, I started polling people in the industry whose opinion I respected, asking if they knew of the alternate formula and why it existed. What I found is that some working production electricians, many of whom have had a long, successful career, have less than a firm grasp of electrical theory. It seems that many people have learned their craft from other, more experienced electricians, who themselves knew little about the concepts behind the application. They know what works in a given situation, they memorize certain numbers and ways of doing things, and they don't deviate for the course of their careers.

A few weeks after this seminar, one of the attendees e-mailed me and told me that he had been discussing the formula with a master electrician. What he concluded, and what he said in the e-mail, is that the entertainment industry is "special" and that the standard formulas "do not really work well" for our applications.

In a way, he's right. Ours is a very specialized industry, and some of the things we do are unique to our industry. For example, when we use dimmer racks in the theatre, we are allowed to size our feeder transformers, feeder cable, and switchgear according to the connected load, rather than the full nameplate rating of the dimmer racks, as would be the case in most every other application. That's because theatres are unique in that they use dimmer-per-circuit systems and not all of the circuits are typically used at any given time.

But our industry is not so different that the laws of nature don't apply! Electrons are still negatively charged, opposite charges still attract, and Ohm's law still applies in every situation, regardless of how unique our industry might be. Therefore, it's vitally important to understand the fundamental relationships that define the nature of electricity. They always apply, regardless of the circumstances.

The fundamental relationships with regards to electricity begin with the atom, how it is structured, how it behaves, and how it works to produce electricity. Once the nature of the atom is understood, then we can begin to understand the relationship between voltage, current, and resistance, which is the fundamental relationship known as Ohm's law. This is the single most important concept that an electrician must grasp. It's the defining relationship that determines so much of what we do.

Also critical to our understanding of electricity are the concepts of power and energy. The two concepts are closely related but distinct. The

understanding of both is as important to the electrician as knowing which tool to use.

Once these concepts are fully understood, then we can start the study of alternating current, or AC. AC differs in many ways from direct current, or DC, although the fundamentals, like Ohm's law, still apply. The difference is that in AC, inductive and capacitive reactance and the element of time come into play.

Understanding AC necessitates the understanding of the average value for a periodic function such as a sinewave. The AC sinewave is critical to understanding many new concepts such as phase angles and power factor.

Calculating power and loads with AC is also more complex than doing so with DC. The formulas for these calculations have to take into account the phase angle or power factor.

After understanding these fundamental relationships we can begin to talk about the components of a power distribution system, how to size them properly for our application, and how to properly connect them. There are several different configurations of electrical service and many different types of connectors that are used to interconnect various components of the system. And although there are several different types and sizes of feeder transformers, they all work in fundamentally the same way. Knowing how to properly size and connect transformers and feeder cable for our application is critical.

Safety is the number one issue when dealing with electrical power distribution, and the disconnect switch and overcurrent protection both play a very important part in that role. They are perhaps the single most important part of designing a safe PD.

After the feeder cable and overcurrent protection typically come the branch circuits or dimmer circuits and the loads. Another critical safety aspect of a distribution system is the grounding system. Each and every circuit must be properly grounded and have a safety grounding wire bonded between conductive metallic enclosures and a grounding rod to ensure the safety of the system. An incorrectly grounded system can be fatal.

Many of the rules that apply to the construction and operation of a power distribution system come from various standard-making bodies around the world. In the United States, the *National Electrical Code* (NEC) and in Canada the Canadian Standards Association set the guidelines that are used by most municipalities throughout the two countries. In the United Kingdom it's the British Standards BS7671: Requirements for Electrical Installations (also known as "the wiring regs"). There are several other standard-making bodies around the world, although there is an ongoing effort to harmonize the standards in the European Union under the International Electrotechnical Commission (IEC) umbrella. The local authorities ultimately have the final jurisdiction, but the code books are often mandated by states or municipalities, sometimes with additional local regulations specific to a locality in order to ensure the health and safety of the general public. Although there are regulations throughout the entire NEC code book that apply to our industry, there are special sections that apply specifically to our needs, including Article 518: Assembly Occupancies; Article 520: Theaters, Audience Areas of Motion Pictures and Television Studios, Performance Areas, and Similar Locations; Article 525: Carnivals, Circuses, Fairs, and Similar Events; and Article 530: Motion Picture and Television Studios, and Similar Locations.

There is much more to know and understand about electricity and electrical power distribution. But understanding the underlying principles will go a long way toward helping you solve problems and puzzle your way through situations. The technology might change over the years, but the basic laws of the universe are unchanging. They stood when we were using gas lamps in the theatre and they stand today when we use automated lights, digital consoles, media servers, and highly networked systems.

ELECTRICITY KILLS, BUT IT DOESN'T HAVE TO

Make no mistake about it: electricity can kill. It takes as little as 60 milliamps (a milliamp is one thousandth of an amp) passing through the heart to make it fibrillate and stop, causing death within a few minutes. And that's not the only way it can kill you. Even if the current doesn't pass directly through your heart, it can contract the muscles in your chest

and asphyxiate you; it can burn you internally; it can damage your brain so much that you can stop breathing.

Fortunately, our skin, which happens to be the largest human organ, provides a relatively high amount of resistance when it is dry. It helps protect us as long as we use common sense, like wearing rubber-soled boots, wearing gloves, and standing on an insulating carpet or rug. On the other hand, risky behavior like standing barefoot on a concrete floor in a puddle of water is asking for trouble.

But the vast majority of fatal accidents involving electricity are not caused by electric shock. They are instead a result of the intense heat and the blast caused by an electrical fault. If you have ever seen video of an arc flash then you understand the potential danger involving high voltage. When switchgear malfunctions or another problem causes a dead short it can create a huge ball of fire with intense heat that engulfs the immediate surroundings and then dissipates in a fraction of a second. In a closed room like a substation or electrical room it can be a deadly situation.

If you understand how electricity behaves and respect its potential for danger, then you can minimize the dangers and work in relative safety. I always wear a pair of gloves and rubber-soled, steel-toe boots when I'm working, not only to protect my hands and feet but also for their insulation value. Most venues do not carpet the areas in which the electrical switchgear is located, so some electricians carry their own rubber matt or carpet to stand on when they are working around live gear or high voltage. These are just a few steps you can take to protect yourself and keep yourself out of harm's way. But you first have to understand the dangers before you can take steps to protect yourself and others from them. There have been far more fatal rigging accidents and pyro accidents in live event production over the past 20 years than there have been fatal electrical accidents. This might be attributed to awareness, education, the constant concern for safety, and perhaps some degree of luck. Never let your guard down.

CHAPTER 1
The Theory of Electricity

"Electricity is really just organized lightning."

George Carlin

WHAT IS ELECTRICITY?

For thousands of years, the nature of electricity puzzled and mystified some of the most brilliant minds. It wasn't until scientists such as Benjamin Franklin, André-Marie Ampère, Alessandro Volta, and Michael Faraday contributed to our understanding of electricity that we began to unlock its secrets. Step by step, bit by bit, we built a plausible model of electricity that fits a mathematical model and provides a real-world explanation of this phenomenon. Even after we had a basic understanding of the key relationships and the fundamentals of electricity, early pioneers such as Joseph Swan, Thomas Edison, Nikola Tesla, and George Westinghouse still struggled to harness its power for daily use in a safe and efficient manner.

During that time — the late 1800s and early 1900s — one of the first practical uses of electricity was to illuminate common areas such as city streets and town squares. New York City quickly became entangled — quite literally — in electrical wires and electricity. Horrified bystanders witnessed the accidental electrocution of several workers in the naked light of day, and electricity gained a reputation for being both mysterious and dangerous. Thomas Edison used the public's fear to protect his economic interests by promoting DC power distribution over AC power distribution, while George Westinghouse grew his business on the

1

strength of AC and its inherent advantages over DC. The ensuing controversy did nothing to ease the public's apprehension about electricity, nor did it help to clarify its nature or promote its understanding.

To this day, many people have little understanding of the nature of electricity. Some of us still have difficulty answering the question, "What is electricity?" After all, we can't see it, hear it, or smell it. And we certainly don't want to taste it or feel it.

An electrician might understand how to hook up a power distribution system but may not fully understand exactly how electricity behaves. By studying the fundamentals of electricity we can better understand how to use electricity safely, effectively, and legally, and we can excel at our jobs in the entertainment industry.

ELECTRONS IN MOTION

The short answer to the question "What is electricity?" is the transfer of energy through the motion of charge-carrying electrons. Lightning is an example of electricity and of electrons — lots and lots of them — in motion. Electricians are generally concerned with a much more controlled situation where electricity flows through a given path in a safe, predictable manner, but the electricity we use in shows is no different than that in a lightning strike, a static discharge, or a flashlight battery. Each is an example of the transfer of energy through the motion of electrons.

But from where do these electrons come? The answer can be found in one of the most basic building blocks of the universe, the atom.

THE ATOM

The word "atom" comes from the Greek word *atomos*, meaning indivisible. It is the smallest particle that still retains the properties of the element from which it comes. If you took your side cutters and cut a small strand of copper from a cable, you would have billions of copper atoms. If you then cut that piece in half, and then in half again, and over and over until you got down to the single piece that still looked and acted like copper, then you would have an atom. But you would have to be pretty good with those cutters. One atom of copper is approximately 10^{-12} meters in diameter. Put another way, it takes about 254 billion copper atoms placed side by side to make 1 inch. Good luck with that.

Atoms are literally everywhere. They make up the air you breathe, the water you drink, the clothes you wear, and the food you eat. They are the building blocks of the universe.

SUBATOMIC PARTICLES

Despite what the early Greeks thought, atoms can be divided. It turns out that they are made up of even smaller subatomic particles called electrons, neutrons, and protons. These sub-atomic particles are very important to the understanding of electricity. Electrons carry a negative charge, protons have a positive charge, and neutrons have no charge at all. It's the interaction of these charges that causes the phenomenon we call electricity.

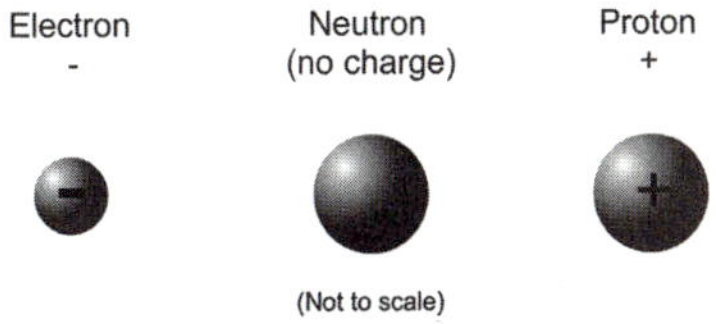

An atom has a nucleus that is made up of a number of protons and neutrons bound by nuclear forces. The nucleus is surrounded by an electron cloud made up of electrons in orbit about the nucleus. The specific number of neutrons, protons, and electrons depends on the element. For example, copper atoms normally have 29 protons, 35 neutrons, and 29 electrons.

ELECTROSTATIC CHARGES

The vast majority of atoms are electrically neutral because the number of negatively charged electrons is balanced by the number of positively charged protons, creating a net charge of zero. In a copper atom, for example, the number of positively charged protons, 29, matches the number of negatively charged electrons; thus the charges cancel each other, resulting in a net charge of zero.

It's important to understand the electrostatic attraction between charges: opposite charges attract and like charges repel. For example, two protons will repel each other and two electrons will repel each other, but a proton will attract an electron.

The force of attraction or repulsion depends on two factors: the magni-tude of the individual charges and the proximity of the charges. The

Electron − Neutron (no charge) Proton +

(Not to scale)

FIGURE 1.1
Atoms are made of three types of particles: electrons, which carry a negative charge; protons, which carry a positive charge; and neutrons, which carry no charge.

3

magnitude of the individual charges, whether they are attracting or repelling, directly affects how strongly the force of attraction or repulsion will be. Since a single proton carries a fixed positive charge and a single electron carries a fixed negative charge, the magnitude of an individual charge depends on the number of protons or electrons involved. An atom with two protons, for example, will have twice the force of attraction to an electron as will an atom with a single proton.

The force of attraction also varies exponentially as the inverse of the distance between the charges. If the distance between the two charges is doubled, then the force of attraction or repulsion will decrease by a factor of four; if the distance is halved, then the force will increase by a factor of four.

$$\text{Force} = k(q_1 \cdot q_2) \div d^2,$$

where force is the magnitude or strength of the force exerted, k is a constant, q_1 and q_2 are charges on the particles, and d is the distance between them.

This relationship shows how the force of attraction or repulsion depends on the magnitude of the two charges, q_1 and q_2, and the distance of separation. This law of attraction or repulsion of electrostatic charges is called Coulomb's law after Charles-Augustin de Coulomb, a French physicist who discovered the relationship.

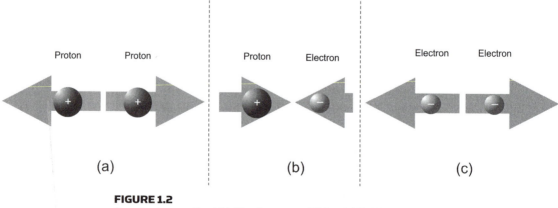

(a)   (b)   (c)

FIGURE 1.2
Opposite charges attract (b); like charges repel [(a) and (c)]. (Not to scale.)

Since opposite charges attract and like charges repel, the electrons in an electron cloud are held in orbit about the nucleus of an atom by their electrostatic attraction to the protons. However, some of the electrons are orbiting so far away from the nucleus that the bond is relatively weak. To give you an idea of the relative distances involved, suppose we could scale our copper atom so that the nucleus was the size of a golf ball. Then you would have to go about 2.41 kilometers (a mile and a half) before you would find the outermost electrons.

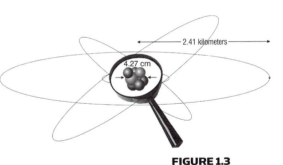

FIGURE 1.3
If the nucleus of an atom were the size of a golf ball, the radius of the orbit of the outermost electrons would be 2.41 kilometers (1.5 miles).

If another external force, like a voltage, is applied, the electrons in the outer orbit can sometimes be pulled away from their associated atom. When that happens, the atom becomes "ionized." The free electrons that are pulled away from the nucleus of an atom can either "drift" toward the force of attraction — from the applied voltage — or they can reassociate with another atom by "falling" into its orbit. An ionized atom that is missing one or more electrons is known as a "hole" in electronics parlance, and it carries a net positive charge.

Every electron carries the same quantity of charge. The coulomb (C) is the standard unit of electric charge as defined by the International System of Units (abbreviated SI for the French *Système International d'Unités*). It is derived from the amount of charge carried by 1 ampere of current in 1 second. It turns out that a single electron carries a charge of -1.6022×10^{-19} coulombs ($-0.00000000000000000016022$ C). Put another way, it takes 6.241506×10^{18} electrons ($6,241,506,000,000,000,000$ electrons) to make 1 coulomb of charge.

ELECTRONIC DRIFT

Some atoms, like copper, silver, and gold, are structured so that their outer electrons are weakly bound to the atom and are more easily pulled from their orbit. Other atoms, like silicon and germanium, have more tightly bonded outer electrons that are less likely to be influenced by external forces. If, for example, we take a length of copper wire and apply a voltage across its ends, the force of attraction between the positive side

5

of the voltage and the negative charge of the weakly bound electrons in the outer orbit can be enough to pull electrons away from the atoms to which they are bound. The free electrons will move in the general direction of the positive voltage because opposite charges attract and like charges repel. The freed electrons migrate through the copper in a random zigzag direction, bumping into other electrons along the way.

When any two objects bump into each other they produce friction, and the friction produces heat. Billions upon billions of electrons are typically flowing in an electrical circuit, and each collision contributes a small amount of heat. That heat represents the loss of energy that is converted from electrical energy and dissipated in the form of heat. Depending on the number of electrons that are flowing and the number of collisions, the total amount of heat loss in the entire circuit can be significant.

The individual electron flowing in a circuit moves only a relatively short distance before it loses kinetic energy and slows down. When it slows down enough, it falls back into the orbit of the closest hole or atom that is missing its outer electron(s). The free electrons move at a relatively slow rate compared to the wave of energy that moves through the copper. It's much like the energy of a sound wave that moves through the air. Individual molecules of air don't travel horizontally with the wave; rather, they compress and decompress as the energy of the wave passes. The air is the medium, but the energy is transferred through it, not with it.

As individual electrons are alternately pulled away from an atom and fall back into the holes, the net result is that they drift across the sea of atoms at a rate of about a few millimeters per second. But the resulting transfer of energy is executed at near the speed of light, which is the speed of electrical transmission.

CONDUCTIVE PROPERTIES OF MATERIALS

In order for current to flow, there must be a conducting medium such as a copper wire, water, air, or some other pathway. Some materials are better conductors of electricity than others because of the structure of

the atoms from which they are made. The atoms in a good conductor more readily give up their electrons in the outer orbit. For that reason, they offer little resistance to the flow of electricity.

Copper, gold, silver, aluminum, and other metallic elements are good conductors. Other materials such as carbon, wood, paper, and rubber are poor conductors of electricity. The atoms from which they are made are structured in a way that requires a lot of energy to pull electrons from their orbit. They are considered good insulators because they inhibit the flow of electricity. Still others, such as germanium and silicon, will conduct electricity under certain conditions. For example, by raising their temperature or placing them in the presence of an electric field we can increase their conductivity. These materials are known as semiconductors.

Table 1.1 shows the resistivity (symbolized by the Greek letter ρ or rho), and its inverse, conductivity (symbolized by the Greek letter σ or sigma), for various materials at the temperature of 20°C. These values are temperature dependent, which is why the temperature must be stated.

7

FIGURE 1.4
A typical utility pole has various conductors and insulators. The copper or aluminum wires and the metal transformer housing are good conductors; the wooden pole and the glass or ceramic insulators are poor conductors.

Table 1.1	Resistivity and Conductivity of Materials at 20°C	
Material	**Resistivity ρ (ohm m)**	**Conductivity σ ($\times 10^7/\Omega$m)**
Silver	1.59×10^{-8}	6.29
Copper	1.68×10^{-8}	5.95
Gold	2.2×10^{-8}	4.5
Aluminum	2.65×10^{-8}	3.77
Tungsten	5.6×10^{-8}	1.79
Iron	9.71×10^{-8}	1.03
Platinum	10.6×10^{-8}	0.943
Solder (63/37 Sn/Pb)	14.4×10^{-8}	0.694
Lead	22×10^{-8}	0.45
Mercury	98×10^{-8}	0.10
Nichrome (Ni, Fe, Cr alloy)	100×10^{-8}	0.10
Carbon (graphite)	$3–60 \times 10^{-5}$	—
Germanium	$1–500 \times 10^{-3}$	—
Silicon	0.1–60...	—
Glass	$1–10\,000 \times 10^9$	—
Quartz (fused)	7.5×10^{17}	—
Hard rubber	$1–100 \times 10^{13}$	—

Source: Giancoli DC. *Physics*. 4th ed. Prentice Hall, Upper Saddle River, New Jersey; 1995.

CURRENT CONVENTION

We started out this chapter by saying that electricity is the transfer of energy through the motion of negatively charged electrons. What, then, is considered to be the direction of the flow of electricity? Is it the same as the direction of the flow of negatively charged electrons, or is it the direction in which a positive charge might flow?

Before very much was known about electricity, current flow was defined to correspond to the flow of positive charges. Since electrons are negatively charged, standard current convention is defined as flowing in the direction opposite electron flow. If it helps to visualize the flow of positively charged particles, then think of the holes as moving in the opposite direction as the electrons; that is the direction of conventional current flow. The primary exception is the U.S. Navy, who uses the opposite current convention.

SUMMARY

Electricity is the transfer of energy through the flow of electrons. Electrons are subatomic particles with a negative charge orbiting about the nucleus of an atom in an electron cloud. The electrons in some atoms are more loosely bound than in other atoms. When an external force such as a voltage is applied to an element with loosely bound electrons in the outermost orbit, the electrons can be pulled free of the atom. Electron drift is the gradual migration of free electrons toward a positive charge. The actual path of individual free electrons is a random zigzag, and the friction produced by bumping into other free electrons produces heat. The free electrons may eventually slow down and fall into a hole, or an atom that is missing an electron. The transfer of energy propagates through the conducting material at a rate approaching the speed of light.

Some materials, such as gold, silver, and copper, are more conductive than others, such as carbon, wood, paper, and rubber. Still others, such as germanium and silicon, can be nonconductors or conductors depending on certain conditions. The direction of current is considered by most people to be opposite the direction of the electron flow.

UNDERSTANDING ELECTRICITY

1.1 What is electricity?

1.2 True or false: The atom is the smallest particle known to humans.

1.3 How small is a single atom of copper?

1.4 What are the three particles found in an atom?

1.5 If an aluminum atom with a net zero charge has 13 protons, how many electrons are there in the electron cloud?

1.6 The force of attraction between a single proton and a single electron is _____ the force of attraction between two protons and one electron.

1.7 The law of attraction or repulsion of electrostatic charges is called _____ _____.

1.8 When an electron is pulled away from the orbit of an atom, the atom becomes _____.

1.9 What is the unit of measure of an electrostatic charge?

1.10 How many electrons does it take to make up 1 coulomb of electrostatic charge?

1.11 Two electrostatic charges are 1 nanometer apart and they have a charge of X coulombs. (a) If one of them carries a negative charge, what is the polarity of the other charge? (b) If the distance between the charges is doubled from 1 nanometer to 2 nanometers, what is the resulting force of attraction?

1.12 Two electrostatic charges that are 8 nanometers apart produce a repelling force of Y newtons. (a) If one of the charges is moved 4 nanometers toward the other, what is the resulting force of repulsion? (b) If the other charge is moved an additional 2 nanometers toward the other, resulting in a separation of 2 nanometers, what is the force of repulsion?

1.13 What is an ionized atom?

1.14 What is the speed of electrical transmission in free air?

1.15 Why is an insulating material unable to easily conduct electricity?

1.16 Which is more conductive, tungsten or iron?

1.17 What is the inverse of resistivity?

1.18 Why is the direction of current convention opposite that of the flow of electrons?

1.19 Is conventional current flow toward or away from the positive terminal of a battery?

CHAPTER 2

Electrical Concepts

"Mystery creates wonder, and wonder is the basis of man's desire to understand."

Neil Armstrong, former American astronaut and the first person to walk on the moon

PULLING BACK THE VEIL OF MYSTERY

Electricity is one of nature's most fascinating phenomena. Its energy can be manifest as light, noise, heat, pressure, or work. It can light up a city, propel cars and buses, and drive any number of appliances that serve to make our lives easier, safer, and more enjoyable. But to a novice, its behavior can be challenging to understand because its characteristics are obscured by a veil of mystery. In Chapter 1 we learned that electricity is the transfer of energy through the flow of electrons. In order to better understand exactly what electricity is and how it behaves, we will want to know its characteristics and fundamental relationships.

There are relatively few concepts that describe the characteristics of electricity, but they are very important to learn. In order to pull back the veil of mystery and truly understand its behavior, it is essential to understand the concepts of voltage, current, resistance, power, and energy, as well as their units of measure.

VOLTAGE

Voltage, or electromotive force (EMF), is what causes electrons to flow through a conductor. It is a potential to push or pull the electrons away from their binding atoms and produce electron drift, transferring energy in the process. Voltage is potential energy, and when it is used to produce electricity, the potential energy is converted to electrical energy. It's similar to the potential energy present when you hold an object in the air. Gravity has the potential to pull the object to the earth, but it doesn't fall unless you allow it to. The force of gravity is potential energy. If you let the object fall, then that potential energy is converted to kinetic energy while it is falling. By the same token, voltage has the potential to make electrons flow through a conductor. Unless there is a closed path along a conductive material through which the electrons can flow, there will be no current flow. But the potential is there.

A battery is an example of an energy storage device that is used to supply a constant voltage to a circuit (as long as it is sufficiently charged). When a battery is charging it is storing energy, and when it is discharging it is supplying energy. If it is charged but not connected to a circuit, then it has the potential to supply energy by applying voltage to it.

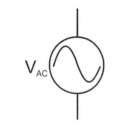

FIGURE 2.1
Schematic diagram for two voltage sources: battery (left) and alternating current or A/C voltage source (right).

Another energy source that supplies a constant voltage is our electrical power grid. It delivers energy from a central generating plant to energy consumers in distant locations. The voltage at the point of consumption varies from 90 or 100 volts in Japan to 120 volts or 208 volts in North America, 230 volts in many parts of Europe and various other locations, and 240 volts in Australia, England, and many other parts of the world.

CURRENT

Current is the flow of electrons or the flow of electrical charges. It is what we understand to be electricity. When a voltage is applied to a conductive material like copper, the electrons are pulled from their outer orbit and drift through the conductor. The result is a transfer of energy from the source to the sink in the form of electrical current.

A voltage can exist without inducing a current, such as when a battery is not connected to a load. In that case, there is no flow of electricity. In order for current to flow there must be a closed path through which electrons can flow. A closed path that can conduct electricity is referred

to as a "complete" circuit or a "closed" circuit. Once a circuit is completed and a current starts flowing, then and only then is there a flow of electricity. If there is a break in a closed circuit that prevents the flow of electricity, it is referred to as an "open" circuit.

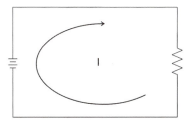

The magnitude of the current flowing in a circuit is one of the main factors that determines how big the components of a power distribution system should be. Once we understand how to calculate the current based on the connected loads and applied voltage, then we can safely configure and operate a power distribution system.

FIGURE 2.2
Current (typically indicated by an arrow in a schematic diagram) can only flow in a complete or closed circuit.

RESISTANCE

Electrical resistance is the opposition to the flow of electric current. A perfect conductor is one in which there is no resistance. In the real world, under normal circumstances, there is no such thing as a perfect conductor; every material has some element of resistance, however small, even the large feeder cables we use for big events. The characteristic resistance of a material is a function of its atomic structure and how many electrons are in its outer orbit. In the real world, the total resistance of cable and wire increases with length, increasing temperature, and decreasing cross-sectional diameter of the conductor. How the resistance in a circuit affects the applied voltage and the amount of current, power, and energy consumed is of great importance to the electrical engineer, electrician, and technician.

POWER

Power is the rate at which work is being done. In physics, work is done when a force is applied over a distance. The rate at which it is applied, that is, the magnitude of the force and the speed at which the distance is covered, determines the amount of power involved. For example, if you and a helper pick up a span of truss from the floor to waist height, you are exerting a mechanical force through a distance; you are doing work. The weight of the truss, and thus the force you apply to counteract the force of gravity, and the speed at which you lift determine the amount of power being applied at any instant in time.

In the case of electric power, the electromotive force (EMF) does work on the negatively charged electrons to move them through a distance. The applied voltage determines the strength of the electric field, and the amount of current is an indicator of how much work is being done. The power, then, is determined by the magnitude of the voltage and current; it is, in fact, the product of the instantaneous voltage and the instantaneous current.

Understanding the power requirements in any given situation is critical to the success of an event. Before the first case is loaded off the truck and before the first rigging point is hung, someone on the crew should have already calculated the power requirements to make sure there is enough power feeding into the building to handle the event and that the power distribution system is able to safely handle the load. It takes a skilled person to understand the power requirements well enough to make that determination.

ENERGY

Energy is a quantity of work done over a period of time, or the capacity to do work. Electricity is a form of energy that can be converted to and from mechanical energy, safely transferred over long distances, harnessed, and used for specific purposes.

Energy and power are two distinct entities. Energy is the product of power and time. To illustrate the difference between the two, suppose that we have two road cases, one weighing 25 kilograms and the other weighing 50 kilograms. It takes twice the power to lift the 50-kilogram case, but it takes the same amount of energy to lift the 25-kilogram road case twice as high. In these cases, the energy expended is equal.

Energy consumption is the largest component of your electricity bill. (The demand factor, which we will discuss later, is the other part of your bill.) Although it is typically a small part of the overall cost of a production, energy efficiency is of great importance to the environment. As good stewards of the earth, it is our responsibility as lighting designers, electrical engineers, electricians, and technicians to understand the ramifications of our design and make the most efficient use, to the extent possible, of our energy. That's not to say that we should compromise the quality of the production for the sake of saving energy, but when given a choice between two options of equal production value, we should take into consideration the environmental impact. Understanding those ramifications requires a good understanding of power and energy.

SI UNITS OF MEASURE: AMPERES, VOLTS, OHMS, SIEMENS, JOULES, WATTS

The International Bureau of Weights and Measures (www.bipm.org) is an international body with 51 member nations that meets every 4 years to establish the convention for weights and measures. In 1960, they adopted the International System of Units (also known as SI units from the French *Le Système International d'Unitès*), in which there are seven base units: the meter, the kilogram, the second, the amp, the kelvin, the mole, and the candela. From those seven base units we can derive several other units. A base unit is one that is standardized by agreement. For example, the length of a meter is defined as the distance light travels in a vacuum in 1/299 792 458 of a second. Derived units are those that can be calculated from their relationship to base units and other derived units. For example, frequency is a derived unit, defined as the inverse of a second (1/second).

The Ampere

Current is one of the seven base units in the SI system. The unit of measure of current is the ampere, or the amp (A). It is named after André-Marie Ampère (1775–1836), a French mathematician and physicist who helped establish the relationship between electricity and magnetism. One amp is defined as the amount of force produced by two current-carrying conductors laid side by side. We will discuss the reasons for this force in more detail later on, but for now, suffice it to say that when a current flows, it creates a magnetic field around the conductor. The magnetic fields of two current-carrying conductors laid side by side in the same orientation will repel each other. The strength of the force of this repulsion is how the SI standard for 1 ampere is measured. One ampere, according to the SI standards, is "that constant current which, if maintained in two straight parallel conductors of infinite length, of negligible cross-section, and placed one meter apart in a vacuum, would produce between these conductors a force equal to 2×10^{-7} newtons per meter of length."

The original definition of an amp was 1 coulomb of charge moving past a point in 1 second. It takes 6.24×10^{18} electrons to produce 1 coulomb of charge. Fortunately, we need not count electrons or measure the strength of magnetic fields in order to measure current in the real world. A clamp meter like the one shown in Figure 2.3 can be used to measure current. It clamps around a current-carrying conductor and measures current by sensing the magnetic field around the conductor.

In electric formulas, current is usually represented in an equation by the letter I. In a schematic diagram, the current is typically indicated by an arrow in the direction of the current.

The Volt

Voltage is a derived unit in the SI system. It is defined as the potential difference across a 1-watt load with a current of 1 amp. The unit of measure of voltage is the volt (V). It is named after Alessandro Volta (1745–1827), an Italian physicist who invented the first modern chemical battery called the voltaic pile. Voltage is sometimes referred to as EMF for electromotive force (most often in physics), but it is most often represented by the letter V.

The Ohm

Electrical resistance is also a derived unit in the SI system. Its unit of measure is called the ohm, after German physicist Georg Ohm (1789–1854). It is abbreviated by the Greek symbol omega (Ω). One ohm is defined as the amount of resistance that will produce a voltage drop of 1 volt given a current of 1 amp. Resistance is usually written as the letter R in an equation.

The Siemens

Conductance is the inverse of resistance, and it is the measure of how easily current flows through a conductor. The unit of measure of conductance is the siemens (G). Until the 14th General Conference on

FIGURE 2.3
A clamp meter allows you to take a variety of measurements, including voltage, current, and resistance.

Weights and Measures adopted the siemens as the unit of measure of conductance in 1971, the unit of measure of conductance was known as the mho.

The Joule

Energy differs from power; energy is power applied over time. The SI unit of measure of energy is the joule. One joule is defined as the work required to move 1 coulomb of charge through a potential difference of 1 volt. Alternatively, a joule is also 1 watt-second, or the amount of energy expended by using 1 watt for 1 second. The joule is named after the English physicist James Prescott Joule (1818–1889).

For our purposes, the joule — a watt-second — is much too small a unit of energy to be practical. A more practical unit of energy is the watt-hour, and that is much more commonly used in the production realm. One watt-hour is the equivalent of 3600 joules. In many cases we will use kilowatt-hours or megawatt-hours as a unit of measure. A thousand watt-hours is equivalent to 1 kilowatt-hour and a million watt-hours is equivalent to 1 megawatt-hour. HVAC (heating, ventilation, and air-conditioning) technicians most often use another unit of energy called the BTU (British thermal unit). This unit of energy will become important when we analyze the impact of a lighting system on the heating of a room.

Each of these units of measure describes a quantity of energy. They are different measures of the same quantity, much like 1 meter is the same as 3.28 feet or 39.37 inches. Regardless of the unit of measure, they can easily be converted from one to another by using the appropriate conversion factor. (See Appendix 3, Energy Conversion Factors.)

The Watt

In the SI system, power is measured in watts, and one watt is defined as one joule per second. The watt is named after James Watt (1736-1819), a Scottish inventor whose improvements to the steam engine helped usher in the Industrial Revolution.

Again, notice that power is not the same as energy, and it is very important to understand the difference between the two. Power is an instan-

taneous measurement of how much work is being done, while energy is a measure of how much force is applied over a distance. Power is usually represented in an equation by the letter *P*.

A NOTE ABOUT UNITS

Units of measure can provide helpful hints when you are solving problems. By looking at the units of measure you can gain valuable insight about the solution. For example, if you want to find out how much energy a particular device is using, the units of energy, watt-hours, tells you that you need to know power of the device in watts, and how many hours it is operating. The symbol • means that you multiply. Suppose we're talking about a 575-watt lamp that runs for 2 hours. The energy consumed will be 575 watts × 2 hours = 1150 watt-hours. Some numbers are unitless, but those with units can give you clues to help you find answers.

Table 2.1	SI Electrical Units of Measure		
Description	**Unit of Measure**	**Abbreviation**	**Description**
Voltage	Volts	V	Potential difference across a 1-watt load with a current of 1 amp
Current	Amperes or amps	A or I	That constant current that, if maintained in two straight parallel conductors of infinite length, of negligible cross-section, and placed 1 meter apart in a vacuum, would produce between these conductors a force equal to 2×10^{-7} newtons per meter of length, or 1 coulomb of charge moving past a point in 1 second
Resistance	Ohms	Ω	The amount of resistance that will produce a drop of 1 volt when 1 amp flows through it
Energy	Joules, watt-hours, kilowatt-hours, or megawatt-hours	J, W-h, kW-h, or MW-h	The amount of work required to move 1 coulomb of charge through a potential difference of 1 volt
Power	Watts, kilowatts, or megawatts	W, kW, or MW	1 joule per second

CONSERVATION OF ENERGY

One of the most important laws of physics is that energy can neither be created nor destroyed. It can change forms — for example, from hydraulic energy to electricity to heat and light and back to heat — but it is always conserved, meaning it can never be lost. This is known as the law of conservation of energy and it is very useful to know when you are calculating energy consumption.

UNDERSTANDING ELECTRICAL CONCEPTS

2.1   Electromotive force (EMF) is also known as _____.

2.2   Voltage is like gravity in which respect?

2.3   In order for a current to flow, there must be voltage and a _____ _____.

2.4   Resistance is the _____ to the flow of current.

2.5   Power is the _____ at which _____ is being done.

2.6   Work is a force applied over a distance. If twice the force is applied over half the distance, is the amount of work done the same?

2.7   If power is voltage times current, is half the voltage and twice the current the same amount of power?

2.8   True or false: Electricity is a form of energy.

2.9   Energy is power times _____.

2.10 According to the law of conservation of energy, energy can neither be _____ nor _____.

2.11 Can current flow in a circuit without voltage?

2.12 In the International System of Units, what are the seven base units?

2.13 The ampere is the unit of measure of _____.

2.14 What is the definition of a volt?

2.15 What is the definition of an ohm?

2.16 The inverse of resistance is _____.

2.17 How many watt-hours are there in 1000 joules?

2.18 How many BTUs does it take to make 1 kilowatt-hour?

CHAPTER 3
DC Electricity

"Electricity is actually made up of extremely tiny particles called electrons, that you cannot see with the naked eye unless you have been drinking."

Dave Barry

Voltage, resistance, and current are not always easy concepts to grasp because electrons are far too small to see. Imagine how our perception of water might change if we couldn't see it. People would appear to magically fly through the air when they were swimming, and ocean waves would appear to be unexplainable forces that could knock you over at seemingly random times. But since we can see water we can easily understand the concepts of water pressure and water flow.

A helpful way to conceptualize electrical concepts is to relate them to a more familiar concept like the flow of water. Water pressure, water flow, and flow resistance in a hydraulic system are very similar to the voltage, current, and resistance in an electric circuit. The water pressure, much like voltage, is the force that pushes water through a pipe. Without it, no water flows. By the same token, without voltage, electrical current will not flow.

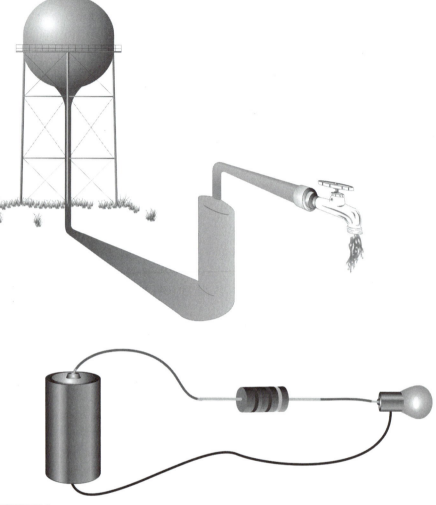

FIGURE 3.1
Top: Water pressure from the tower forces water through the pipe, the flow restrictor limits the amount of water that runs through the pipe, and the flow valve turns the water on and off. Bottom: In a DC circuit, the voltage supplied by a battery drives current through the wires in much the same way that the water pressure forces the water through the pipes. A resistor in a DC circuit limits the flow of electricity and a light bulb draws the current.

The amount of water that flows through a pipe is analogous to the amount of current flowing in a conductor, and the pipe is analogous to the conductor. The bigger the pipe, the easier the water flows; the smaller the pipe, the less water can flow. A small pipe, then, is analogous to a small conductor or a conductor with a high resistance. A large pipe is analogous to a large conductor or a conductor with low resistance.

A complete water distribution system is analogous to an electric circuit. The water stored in a reservoir is like a battery with a stored charge. A tank that holds water high off the ground produces a tremendous amount of water pressure, much like the "electrical pressure," or voltage in a battery, ready to deliver water or electricity on demand. The pipe that carries water to a subdivision is like the wire that carries electricity from the battery to a light bulb. Along the way there are switches and valves that turn the water or electricity on and off. When the tap is on, the water flows, and when the light switch is on, the current flows.

THE DC CIRCUIT

A simple direct current (DC) circuit is shown in Figure 3.2. A battery provides the voltage that makes the current flow, provided there is a complete path of conductive material, like copper wire, from one terminal of the battery to the other. The wiring provides such a path, which completes the circuit. If there is no wire, or if the wire does not return to the other terminal, then it is an incomplete circuit.

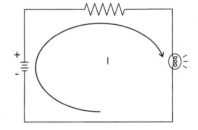

FIGURE 3.2
Schematic diagram of a DC circuit.

In addition to a battery and a lamp, the circuit also has a resistor. The function of the resistor is to limit the amount of current flowing through the circuit. Without it, the only factors limiting the current are the size of the copper wire, the resistance of the lamp filament, and the voltage of the battery. If the circuit resistance is too low, a very large current will flow and the wire and lamp filament will heat up, possibly to the point of destruction. The resistor prevents that from happening. The load in this case is a lamp, but it might just as easily be a fog machine or anything that uses electricity.

SI PREFIXES AND NOTATION

Very large and very small numbers are often abbreviated using prefixes, scientific notation, or exponential notation, as a matter of convenience. SI prefixes are standardized according to the International Systems of Units, and are listed in Table 3.1. For example, kilo is a prefix meaning 1000; therefore, a kilowatt is 1000 watts.

Scientific notation is written as a mathematic exponential expression using a coefficient, powers of ten and an exponent in the form $a \times 10^b$. The coefficient a can be any number, and the exponent indicates the power of ten. For example, $1 \times 10^3 = 1 \times 10 \times 10 \times 10 = 1000$. Therefore, 2 kilowatts may be expressed in scientific notation as 2×10^3 watts. In this example, the number "3" is the exponent and "2" is the coefficient.

A negative exponent indicates that you divide by 10 rather than multiply by 10. For example, $1 \times 10^{-3} = 1 \div 10 \div 10 \div 10 = 0.001$.

Exponential notation is similar to scientific notation except the power of ten is not shown as a superscript or raised digit. Instead, it is replaced with the letter "E" or "e," for exponent, and the power of ten. For example, instead of expressing 2 kilowatts as 2×10^3, it can be expressed as 2E3, 2E+3 or 2e+3, where "E" or "e" represents "$\times 10$ raised to the power of." E notation is often used on calculators and meters where the display is limited to a few digits. Notice that a positive exponent indicates that the decimal place moves to the right, and a negative exponent indicates that the decimal place moves to the left. For example, $2 \times 10^{-3} = 0.002$, while $2 \times 10^3 = 2000$.

Engineering notation is similar to exponential notation except the exponent is limited to powers of three. Thus, in engineering notation, we can speak of watts, kilowatts, and megawatts, but not 2×10^4 watts. Exponents that are multiples of three correspond to the prefixes nano (10^{-9}), micro (10^{-6}), milli (10^{-3}), kilo (10^3), mega (10^6), and giga (10^9).

OHM'S LAW

Ohm's law is one of the most important and useful fundamental relationships in electricity and electronics. If you have a good understanding of what it means and how to use it, then you will have taken a large step toward demystifying electricity and electronics. Much of what we will learn throughout this book is based on Ohm's law and its derivations.

Ohm's law describes the relationship between voltage, current, and resistance. It simply says that voltage is the product of current and resistance.

$$\text{Ohm's law}: V \,(\text{volts}) = I \,(\text{amps}) \times R \,(\text{ohms})$$

	Scientific Notation	Exponential Notation	Engineering Notation	Decimal Equivalent
SI Prefix				
Pico	10^{-12}	E-12	10^{-12}	0.000 000 000 001
Nano	10^{-9}	E-9	10^{-9}	0.000 000 001
Micro	10^{-6}	E-6	10^{-6}	0.000 001
Milli	10^{-3}	E-3	10^{-3}	0.001
Centi	10^{-2}	E-2	n/a	0.01
Deci	10^{-1}	E-1	n/a	0.1
—	10^{0}	E+0	n/a	1
Deca	10^{1}	E+1	n/a	10
Hecto	10^{2}	E+2	n/a	100
Kilo	10^{3}	E+3	10^{3}	1000
Mega	10^{6}	E+6	10^{6}	1,000,000
Giga	10^{9}	E+9	10^{9}	1,000,000,000
Tera	10^{12}	E+12	10^{12}	1,000,000,000,000

Table 3.1   SI Prefixes and Corresponding Notation

25

What this tells us is that for a given resistance, the current is directly proportional to the voltage: the higher the voltage, the higher the current and vice versa. Alternatively, for a given voltage, the current is inversely proportional to the resistance in a circuit: the higher the resistance, the lower the value of the current.

Example 3a

What is the voltage needed to produce 2 amps in a 100-ohm resistor?

Answer:

$$V = I \times R$$

$$V = 2 \times 100$$

$$V = 200 \text{ volts}$$

Remember to always include the unit of measure to make sure your answer is understood properly.

With Ohm's law, we can use any two of the three values — voltage, current, or resistance — to determine the missing value. By manipulating the formula $V = I \times R$, we can come up with two other useful variations:

$$I = V/R$$

$$R = V/I$$

Example 3b

In a 12-volt DC circuit, how much current would flow through a 150-ohm resistor?

Answer:

$$I = V/R$$

$$I = 12/150$$

$$I = 80 \text{ milliamps (0.08 amps)}$$

Example 3c

What is the resistance of a cable that allows 10 amps to flow through it when a 24-volt battery is applied to it?

Answer:

$$R = V/I$$

$$R = 24 \div 10$$

$$R = 2.4 \text{ ohms}$$

DC POWER

We've already learned that power is the rate at which work is being done. When it comes to electricity, work is being done any time current is flowing. The greater the flow of current, the more work that is being done. The same can be said of the voltage: the higher the voltage, the more work that is being done (assuming there is a complete circuit and current is flowing).

In a DC circuit, the power in watts is equal to the voltage times the current. For a fixed voltage, a higher current means that more power is being used, and for a fixed current, a higher voltage also means that more power is being used.

The power formula for a DC circuit can be expressed in terms of the voltage and current as follows:

$$P(\text{watts}) = V(\text{volts}) \times I(\text{amps})$$

Example 3d

If we connect a 12-volt battery to a lamp, measure the current, and find that it draws 1 amp, how much power is consumed?

Answer:

$$P = V \times I$$

$$P = 12 \text{ volts} \times 1 \text{ amp}$$

$$P = 12 \text{ watts}$$

The power formula can also be expressed in terms of voltage and resistance. We can use Ohm's law to substitute the equivalent of the current into the power formula.

$$P(\text{watts}) = V(\text{volts}) \times I(\text{amps})$$

$$P = V \times [V \div R]$$

$$P = V^2 \div R$$

Example 3e

If a lamp is rated 500 watts at 12 volts, what is the effective resistance of the filament at its operating temperature? (The resistance of the filament changes with its temperature.)

Answer:

$$P = V^2 \div R$$

$$500 = 12^2 \div R$$

$$R = 144 \div 500$$

$$R = 0.288\,\text{ohms}$$

By manipulating the power formula, we can rearrange it to solve for voltage or current as follows:

$$V\,(\text{volts}) = P\,(\text{watts}) \div I\,(\text{amps})$$

or

$$I\,(\text{amps}) = P\,(\text{watts}) \div V\,(\text{volts})$$

Power can also be expressed purely in terms of current and resistance. By using Ohm's law, we can substitute for the voltage:

$$P\,(\text{watts}) = V\,(\text{volts}) \times I\,(\text{amps})$$

$$P = [I \times R] \times I$$

$$P = I^2 \times R$$

What this formula tells us is that, regardless of the voltage, there is a definite relationship between the power, current, and resistance. It not only allows us to make power calculations, but it also reveals a very important fact about the efficiency of a system. It says that, for a given amount of current, there is a certain amount of power that is lost to parasitic resistance in the system. The resistance can come from the characteristics of the copper in the cable, the connection points throughout the system, or other sources. The lost power is proportional to the resistance in the circuit and to the square of the current flowing through it. The loss of power due to resistance is known as the I²R loss (pronounced I-squared R).

This is important because parasitic resistance in a circuit can significantly degrade its efficiency. In every circuit there is some value, however small or large, of parasitic resistance, or resistance not intentionally built into the system. For example, in a typical entertainment power distribution and dimming system, the parasitic resistance causes I²R losses in feeder transformers, cables, connectors, dimmers, and loads. Since there is no such thing as a perfect conductor, every conductor has some amount of resistance, however small. This resistance contributes to I²R losses.

Example 3f

If a 20-amp branch circuit is wired with 500 feet of 12-gauge stranded copper wire (250 feet to the load and 250 feet back to the panel) and the resistance of the wire is 1.588 ohms per 1000 feet, calculate the power lost to the resistance of the wire (called the I^2R loss) using the power formula above.

Answer:

$$P = I^2 \times R$$

We know the maximum current is 20 amps, and the total resistance of the branch circuit is half of 1.588 ohms, or 0.794 ohms. Therefore,

$$P = (20\,\text{amps})^2 \times 0.794 = 400 \times 0.794$$

$$P = 317.6\,\text{watts}$$

Finding the voltage, current, resistance, or power is simply a matter of examining the known values and using the right formula to calculate the unknown value. The chart in Figure 3.3 is useful for identifying the knowns and the unknowns and for choosing the right formula.

Power in an AC circuit is not as straightforward as in a DC circuit because of the nature of alternating current. We will discuss AC power later on in this book.

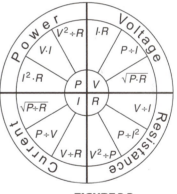

FIGURE 3.3
Voltage, resistance, current, and power formulas.

UNDERSTANDING DC ELECTRICITY

3.1   In a 24-volt circuit, a lamp draws 6.25 amps. What is the effective resistance of the lamp?

3.2   A 12-volt circuit has a 3-amp fuse. How much resistance is required to keep the fuse from blowing?

3.3   If a current of 10 amps is flowing through a 150-ohm resistor, what is the voltage drop across the resistor?

3.4   If a 9-volt battery is connected to an axial fan and it draws 100 milliamps, what is the resistance of the fan?

3.5   A 24-volt circuit is connected to a 150-ohm heating element. How much current will flow?

3.6   A current of 5 amps is flowing through a circuit with a 9-volt battery. What is the resistance in the circuit?

3.7   A 24-volt battery is connected to two 100-ohm resistors in series. If a current of 0.12 amps is flowing through the circuit, what is the equivalent resistance of the two resistors in series?

3.8   A load draws a current of 6 amps when a 12-volt battery is connected to it. If the voltage is increased to 24 volts, how much current will flow through it?

3.9   If a 12-volt battery produces a 500-milliamp current, what is the resistance of the circuit?

3.10 How many millivolts would it take to produce a 10-milliamp current in a circuit with resistance of 10 ohms?

3.11 A 12-volt bulb draws 10 amps at the rated voltage. What is the rated power of the bulb?

3.12 A lamp is rated 150 watts at 12 volts. How many amps will it draw at the rated voltage?

3.13 How much current is drawn by a lamp rated 250 watts at 24 volts?

3.14 If a lamp is rated 60 watts at 12 volts, what is the resistance of the filament at the operating temperature?

3.15 If a resistor dissipates 100 watts at 12 volts, how much power will it use if it is connected to a 9-volt power supply? (Hint: find the value of the resistor, then the current at 9 volts.)

3.16 Write the following number in scientific notation: 2,350,000.

3.17 Write the following number in long form: 5.66×10^{-6}.

3.18 Write the following number in engineering notation: 8.125 megawatts.

CHAPTER 4

AC Electricity

"I have just seen the drawings and descriptions of an electrical machine lately patented by a Mr. Tesla, and sold to the Westinghouse Company, which will revolutionize the whole electric business in the world. It is the most valuable patent since the telephone."

Mark Twain, November 1888*

Alternating current is made possible by the principle of rotating magnetic fields. In fact, without magnetism, there would be no electricity at all. In order to fully understand how AC electricity is generated, distributed, and used, we must first understand its underlying principles, starting with magnetism.

MAGNETISM

Rare is the person who has not played with a magnet or two and doesn't know that magnetism is the phenomenon of attraction or repulsion between two materials. But how many of us know what causes magnetism?

As we learned in Chapter 1, atoms are made up of electrons, protons, and neutrons. In addition to carrying an electrostatic charge, electrons

---

*From *Edison to Enron: The Business of Power and What It Means for the Future of Electricity*, Richard Munson (Praeger Publishers, 2005).

also exhibit what is known as a magnetic dipole. This is an intrinsic property of every electron that produces a magnetic field with a particular strength and orientation. The orientation of the magnetic field is always from the north pole to the south pole. Ordinarily, groups of electrons are randomly aligned and their magnetic fields cancel. But in certain materials, the electrons are ordered in such a manner that the magnetic fields reinforce each other, resulting in residual magnetism, the strength of which depends on the number of unpaired electrons available to be realigned.

In some materials like magnetite, unpaired electrons spontaneously align themselves and reinforce the magnetic field. When that happens in permanent magnets it is referred to as ferromagnetism. In other materials such as aluminum, the material is only magnetic in the presence of an external magnetic field. This type of magnetism is referred to as paramagnetism.

Magnets behave in a manner similar to electrostatic charges: like poles repel, unlike poles attract, and the strength of repulsion or attraction varies inversely with the square of the distance separating them. The lines of force about a magnet describe the strength and direction of the magnetic field. Although the magnetic field is invisible, its effects can be seen by sprinkling iron filings on a clear glass surface and placing a magnet under the glass, as shown in Figure 4.1.

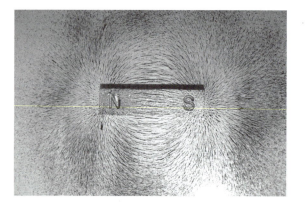

FIGURE 4.1
Iron filings indicating the magnetic lines of force surrounding a common magnet. The direction of the lines of force is from the south pole to the north pole.

ELECTROMAGNETISM

In the early nineteenth century, very little was known about electricity. One day in the spring of 1820, a Danish physicist named Hans Christian Øersted, who taught at Copenhagen University, stumbled upon a previously unknown phenomenon. While he was giving a lecture about the heat generated by a current flowing through a platinum wire, he noticed something that he did not expect. A compass happened to be on his desk in the vicinity of the wire, and when the current flowed he noticed that the needle deflected. He had discovered that electricity and magnetism were inextricably linked.*

We already know that electrons carry an electrostatic charge and that electricity is the flow of electrons. Since the discovery of electromagnetism, we understand that electric current also produces a magnetic field

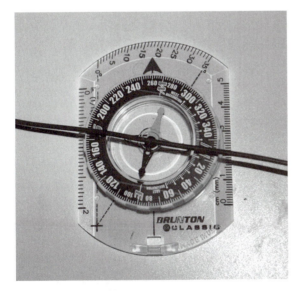

FIGURE 4.2
Electricity and magnetism are inextricably linked.

*In 1802, an amateur physicist named Gian Domenico Romagnosi conducted experiments and wrote about the relationship between electricity and magnetism. The results were published in two local Italian journals, but they never attracted the attention of the scientific community. By contrast, Øersted's literature about his discovery was translated from its original Latin and widely circulated among the European scientific community. Consequently, Øersted is commonly credited with the discovery.

(electromagnetism). If we could see the lines of flux of that electromagnetic field, we would see concentric rings around the current-carrying conductor falling off in strength as they get farther from the conductor. Following what is known as the right-hand rule, we can visualize the direction of the magnetic lines of flux by taking our right hand and wrapping our fingers around the conductor with our thumb protruding along the conductor, pointing in the direction of the current flow. Our fingers will then indicate the direction of the magnetic lines of flux, as shown in Figure 4.3. The strongest magnetic field is closest to the conductor, and the strength is inversely proportional to the square of the distance from the conductor; for example, if the distance from the conductor doubles, then the strength of the magnetic field drops off by a factor of four.

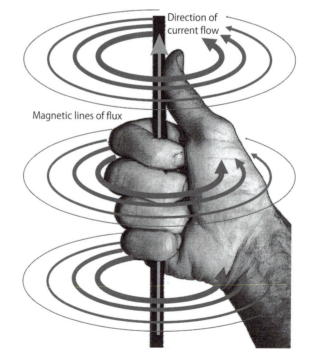

Direction of current flow

Magnetic lines of flux

FIGURE 4.3
The magnetic field produced by the flow of current is electromagnetism. If you grasp a conductor with your right hand and point your thumb in the direction of the current flow, your fingers will indicate the direction of the magnetic lines of flux.

MAGNETIC INDUCTION

If an electric current creates a magnetic field, can a magnetic field induce the flow of current through a wire? That was the question that was on the mind of English scientist Michael Faraday one day in 1822 when he wrote in his laboratory notebook, "Convert magnetism into electricity."*

By 1822, it was known that electricity and magnetism were inextricably linked. It was easy to see the link by the deflection of a compass needle in the proximity of a current-carrying wire, and it was known that the field could be strengthened by wrapping multiple turns of wire in a coil. But few people had an inkling that you could actually generate electricity by using magnetism. Faraday was one of those who thought it could be done, and for a long time he tried unsuccessfully to do just that.

It wasn't until 9 years later, in 1831, that he happened upon a clue. He had wrapped one side of an iron toroid with several turns of wire and on the other side he did the same. One of the conductors was connected to a battery and the other was connected to a galvanometer (or an amp meter) so he could detect the flow of current. He wanted the magnetic field in the first coil to somehow induce the current to flow in the second coil. But when he connected the battery and made current flow in the primary coil, there was no current in the secondary coil. What he did notice, however, is that the meter deflected momentarily when the battery was first connected.

FARADAY'S LAW OF INDUCTION

The famous author Isaac Asimov once said, "The most exciting phrase to hear in science, the one that heralds new discoveries, is not 'Eureka!' (I found it!) but, 'That's funny. …'" That might have been what Faraday

---

*Empires of Light: Edison, Tesla, Westinghouse, and the Race to Electrify the World, Jill Jonnes (Random House, 2003).

thought when he noticed the meter deflection upon connecting and disconnecting the battery. Even though he didn't get the result he was looking for — current flowing steadily through the secondary coil — he did see a hint of current flow in the form of a slight needle deflection in the galvanometer. But it was enough to lead him down the right path to the answer. Eventually, he found that a stationary magnetic field does not induce current in the secondary coil, but that a changing magnetic field does.

When a battery is first connected to a circuit, the magnetic field has to build from zero to its maximum. As the field grows, the lines of flux of the magnetic field cut the turns of wire in the secondary coil, thereby inducing a current. Faraday deduced that a changing magnetic field whose lines of flux cut through a wire will generate a voltage. The value of the voltage is proportional to the rate of change and the intensity of the magnetic flux. This is known as Faraday's law of induction.

According to Faraday's law of induction, it doesn't matter whether the lines of flux are cutting through the wire or the wire is moving through the lines of flux, as long as they are moving relative to each other. Therefore, a wire can move through a stationary magnetic field or a magnetic field can move through a stationary wire and it will still generate voltage.

What is important is that the wire is not moving parallel relative to the lines of flux (0°), otherwise no lines of flux will be cut and no voltage will be generated. The movement can, however, be somewhere in between parallel and perpendicular (90°) relative to each other; then some lines of flux will be cut and a proportional amount of voltage will be generated. For example, if a wire is moving at a 60° angle through a magnetic field, then it is cutting half as many lines of flux as another wire traveling at a 90° angle to the magnetic field at the same rate of speed. Therefore, it would generate half the voltage.

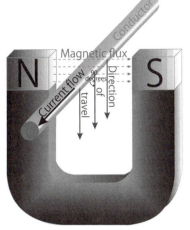

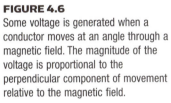

FIGURE 4.4
Voltage is induced in a conductor when it moves at a right angle to a magnetic field.

FIGURE 4.5
Voltage is not induced when a conductor moves parallel to a magnetic field.

FIGURE 4.6
Some voltage is generated when a conductor moves at an angle through a magnetic field. The magnitude of the voltage is proportional to the perpendicular component of movement relative to the magnetic field.

FLEMING'S RIGHT-HAND RULE

37

The direction current travels or the polarity of the voltage generated in a conductor as it moves through a magnetic field is important to know. When the conductor is moving in one direction, the polarity is opposite that of a conductor moving the other direction.

In order to remember the relative direction of current induced by a conductor moving through a magnetic field, you can use Fleming's right-hand rule for generators (as opposed to Fleming's left-hand rule for motors). Using your right hand, stick out your thumb in the direction of the travel of the conductor, extend your index finger in the direction of the magnetic flux (north to south) and hold your middle finger out so that it is at a right angle relative to both your index finger and your thumb. Your middle finger indicates the direction of the flow of induced current in a generator. To remember which finger relates to which parameter, it helps to use this mnemonic: thuMb = Motion; First finger = Field (or Flux); and seCond finger = Current. Fleming's left-hand rule applies to motors.

FIGURE 4.7
Fleming's right-hand rule for generators helps to determine the direction of an induced current.

How does all of this relate to supplying power for a show? It has to do with the way electricity is generated and used. A generator typically has a magnetic rotor that spins in close proximity to stationary windings that cut the lines of flux and generate electricity.

THE AC GENERATOR

Although it took more than 50 years, Faraday's law laid the foundation for building electrostatic generators, transformers, and motors. Once it was established that a conductor moving through a magnetic field can induce a current, building a generator was a relatively simple matter of assembling the components properly.

To illustrate, suppose we have an axle about which we want to build a generator. We can either make the magnetic field spin around a stationary coil of wire, or we can make the coil spin through a magnetic field. Either way, the important thing is that there is relative motion between the coil of wire and the magnetic field. It's easier to illustrate a stationary magnetic field and a spinning coil of wire, so we'll use that model for our illustration.

Let's start by bending some wire in a rectangular shape so that two of the sides of the loop are perpendicular to the magnetic field and the other two are parallel. We'll call this the rotor because it rotates about the center. On one end of the loop we can add two leads that connect to slip rings that allow us to tap into the circuit.

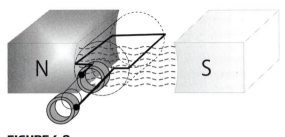

FIGURE 4.8
A loop of wire in a magnetic field illustrates the basic concept of the alternating current generator.

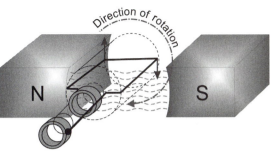

FIGURE 4.9
As the loop of wire spins, it cuts through the magnetic lines of flux. The two arrows show the instantaneous direction of travel.

As the rotor spins, the two sides of the conductor that cut the lines of flux rotate 360° through the magnetic field in one full cycle. Along the way, their instantaneous direction of travel at any particular time is indicated by a line that is at a right angle to the radius of travel (see Figure 4.9).

During each cycle, there are four critical points of interest that will help us visualize the generator concept: 0°, 90°, 180°, and 270°. At the instant in time when the rotor and conductors are at the top of the circle (0°), the direction of travel is parallel to the lines of flux, so no voltage is generated. After the rotor has spun 90°, the conductors are traveling at a right angle to the flux and generate the peak voltage. At 180° the conductors are traveling in the opposite direction relative to the start of the cycle; but since the instantaneous direction of travel is parallel to the flux, no voltage is generated. Then at 270°, they are traveling in the opposite direction as they were at the 90° point; therefore, it generates a negative voltage. When the rotor completes one full cycle, it returns to its original starting point and the voltage drops to zero again.

In between these four critical points the voltage varies according to the sine* of the angle between the instantaneous direction of travel and the magnetic lines of flux. The instantaneous voltage is given below:

$$V_{instantaneous} = V_{peak} \times \sin \theta$$

*Sine is a math function that relates an angle of a right triangle (a triangle with one 90° angle) to the ratio of two of its sides.

39

where θ is the angle between the instantaneous direction of travel and the magnetic lines of flux. For example, if the rotor is straight up and down, then the instantaneous direction of travel is parallel to the magnetic lines of flux and the angle between them is 0°. If we use a trigonometric calculator, we can find the value of the sine of 0°, which is 0; so the instantaneous voltage is also 0. But when the rotor rotates 30°, then the sine is 0.5, so the voltage is half of the peak voltage.

Figure 4.10 shows several rotor positions and the associated voltage generated by the relative motion of the coil and the magnetic field.

If we chart several points in a single rotation starting at the top of the circle, we can plot the voltage for the entire cycle. You can verify the values in Table 4.1 by using a calculator and finding the sine of each of the values in the middle column.

Table 4.1	Rotor Position, Phase Angle, and Voltage Multiplier	
Rotor Position in Degrees	Angle between Direction of Travel and Magnetic Lines of Flux (Also Known as the Phase Angle)	Voltage Multiplier (Sine of Angle between Direction of Travel and Magnetic Lines of Flux)
90	0	0
60	30	0.5
30	60	0.866
0	90	1
−30	120	0.866
−60	150	0.5
−90	180	0
−120	210	−0.5
−150	240	−0.866
−180	270	−1
−210	300	−0.866
−240	330	−0.5
−270	360	0

Step	Illustration	Rotor position	Direction of travel	Sine of angle
1.			→ = 0	0.0
2.			↘ = 30	0.5
3.			↓ = 90	1.0
4.			↙ = 120	0.866
5.			← = 180	0.0
6.			↖ = 210	-0.5
7.			↑ = 225	-1.0
8.			↗ = 255	-0.866

FIGURE 4.10

As the rotor spins, the angle between the instantaneous direction of travel and the magnetic field determines the magnitude of the voltage generated. The sine of the angle times the peak voltage is the instantaneous voltage.

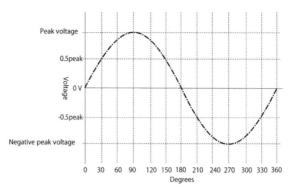

FIGURE 4.11
A plot of the rotor position in degrees versus the voltage shows a waveform known as a sinewave.

If we now plot the values of voltage in Table 3.1, we can connect the dots and see the entire voltage waveform (Figure 4.11). This is known as a sinewave. Notice in Table 4.1 and Figure 4.11 that the angle between the direction of travel and the magnetic lines of flux is what is known as the phase angle. For example, the positive peak voltage occurs at a phase angle of 90°.

The exact voltage at any point in the waveform can be found if we know the peak voltage:

$$V_{instantaneous} = V_{peak} \times \sin \theta$$

where θ is the phase angle. Don't let the word "sine" trip you up. It is really nothing more than the fixed relationship between an angle and the sides of a right triangle. In the abstract, trigonometry can be challenging, but in real-world applications it can be useful to help visualize important relationships.

EXERCISE YOUR KNOWLEDGE OF SINEWAVES

Microsoft Excel is an excellent resource for helping us understand certain natural relationships and for reinforcing what we've learned about sinewaves and voltage waveforms. Using a computer with Excel, follow the directions below to create a sinewave and chart.

1. Open a new workbook.

2. In cell A1, enter a "0."

3. Drag the fill handle (in the lower right-hand corner of cell A1) down to cell A361.

4. In the menu, click on Edit, then Fill, then Series. A window should open as shown in Figure 4.12.

5. Click "OK." The window should close, and cells A1 through A361 should automatically fill with values from 0 through 360. These values represent the phase angle.

6. In cell B1, enter the following formula minus the quotes and the period at the end: "= SIN(RADIANS(A1))." This is the formula for the sine of the value in cell A1, which is our starting phase angle. The reason we included the term "RADIANS" is because Excel is formatted to interpret polar values in terms of radians rather than degrees. By using the conversion formula, we've indicated that the phase angle in cell A1 is in degrees rather than radians.

7. Drag the fill handle (in the lower right-hand corner of cell B1) down to cell B361. That will copy the formula in cell B1 to each of the cells down to B361, replacing cell A1 with the respective cell to its left. For example, in cell B2, the formula "= SIN(RADIANS(A1))" will be replaced with "= SIN(RADIANS (A2))." Leave the cells highlighted.

8. With the cells still highlighted, click on Insert in the menu, and then Chart. This should open the Chart Wizard as shown in Figure 4.13.

9. In Chart type, click on Line, and then click Finish. It will create a graphic of your sinewave, as shown in Figure 4.14.

10. Save your file for future exercises.

Series   ⁇✗

Series in
○ Rows
● Columns

Type
● Linear
○ Growth
○ Date
○ AutoFill

Date unit
● Day
○ Weekday
○ Month
○ Year

□ Trend

Step value: 1   Stop value:

OK   Cancel

FIGURE 4.12
Series window.

43

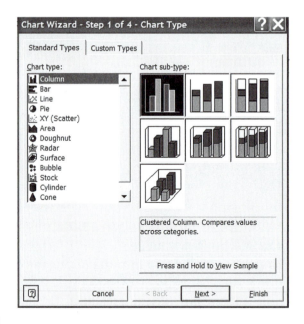

FIGURE 4.13
Chart Wizard.

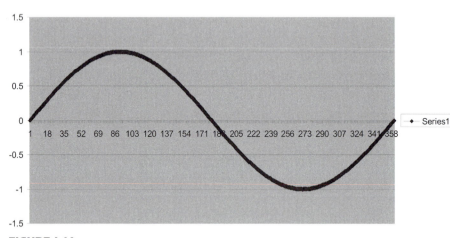

FIGURE 4.14
Sinewave graphic.

FREQUENCY

The generator we "built" in this chapter is an example of a two-pole machine; it has one north and one south magnetic pole. It's also a synchronous generator, meaning that the position and speed of the rotor are synchronized with the voltage waveform: the faster the rotation, the faster the voltage waveform repeats. The speed at which the wave repeats is called the frequency. In real life, synchronous generators rotate at relatively constant speed with slight variations caused by changes in the connected load.

Some generators have more than two poles. Commercial power generators that are commonly used with fossil fuels, nuclear reactors, and hydraulic turbines are synchronous generators, but they are designed with different numbers of poles depending on how fast they can rotate.

A two-pole fossil fuel steam turbine can operate at a high rate of speed, typically 3000 revolutions per minute in Europe or 3600 rpm in North America. A nuclear steam turbine typically runs at half that speed and has four poles in order to produce the same frequency. But hydroelectric generators, which have enormous turbine blades and reciprocating engine generators, like diesel generators, spin at lower speeds and therefore need more poles to produce the same waveform as higher RPM generators. Some hydroelectric generators operate at speeds as slow as 100 or 120 RPM with 60 poles.*

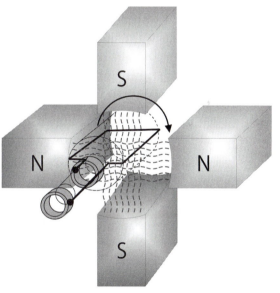

FIGURE 4.15
A four-pole generator operating at half the speed of a two-pole generator produces the same frequency.

From these examples we can see that, in order to produce the same frequency, the speed of rotation of a generator is inversely proportional to the number of poles in the machine; the higher the speed, the fewer the number of poles.

*Standard Handbook for Electrical Engineers, 15th edition, H. Wayne Beaty and Donald G. Fink, (McGraw-Hill, 2007).

45

$$\text{Speed of rotation of generator (RPM)} \sim \frac{1}{poles}$$

The speed of rotation in a synchronous machine is also directly proportional to the number of times the voltage waveform repeats every second, which is called the frequency. Frequency is expressed in units of hertz (Hz), named after the German physicist Heinrich Hertz. Sixty RPM is equal to 1 Hz.

$$\text{Speed of rotation of generator (RPM)} \sim \text{frequency (Hz)}$$

If we combine the two relationships above, we get the following:

$$\text{Speed of rotation (RPM)} \times \text{number of poles} = 120 \times \text{frequency (Hz)}$$

Frequency is an important concept in AC electricity. It affects the operation of magnetic power supplies for discharge lamps, the interaction of video and film, and the operation of some electronics. In most of North America and Central America and parts of South America, the frequency of the voltage is standardized at 60 Hz; in Australia and most of Europe it is 50 Hz.

THE SINEWAVE

Until now we have avoided referring to any specific magnitude or value of voltage in the AC waveform. Instead, we have been referring to the peak value or maximum value of the sinewave. But there are two voltage values of interest in power distribution: the peak and the root mean square (RMS) value.

When we are talking about AC voltage, we are generally referring to the RMS value. If it's not specified whether we're talking about the RMS or the peak value (and most of the time it isn't specified), then the RMS is implied. In a sinewave, the RMS value is a function of the peak value, so if we know the peak value we can calculate the RMS value and vice versa.

In a sinewave, the voltage fluctuates between the positive value of the maximum voltage and the negative value of the maximum voltage at a rate specified by the frequency. If, for example, the peak is 169.73 volts, then the AC voltage fluctuates between +169.73 volts and −169.73 volts.

RMS VALUE

But what, exactly, is the root mean square, or the RMS? It's a way of evaluating the equivalent power transferred to a load with a given voltage. It is not the average voltage; the average voltage of an AC system doesn't convey enough information. For example, suppose we had a series of numbers and we wanted to average them. Normally, we would add them up and divide the result by the number of digits we averaged. Let's take the average value of these four numbers: 0, 50, 80, and 100. The average is $(0 + 50 + 80 + 100) \div 4 = 230 \div 4 = 57.5$. Now suppose we had another group of numbers: 0, −50, −80, and −100. The average of these four numbers is −57.5. If we combined the two groups of numbers and averaged them, what would be the result?

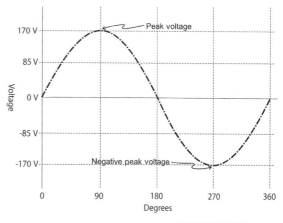

FIGURE 4.16
In an AC waveform, the voltage fluctuates between the positive maximum voltage and the negative value of the maximum voltage.

$$(0+50+80+100-0-50-80-100)\div 8 = 0 \div 8 = 0$$

$$\text{Average} = 0$$

A sinewave is much like these two groups of numbers in that the positive half cycle and the negative half cycle average to zero over the entire cycle. But if we were to touch a live wire with alternating current, we would instantly recognize that the average value over a cycle doesn't convey enough information! A much more meaningful measure of a periodic function like a sinewave is the RMS value.

RMS literally means the square root of the average, or mean, of the squares of the numbers. That simply means that if we take the square of each value in a series of numbers, find the average of those numbers, and then take the square root of the result, we will have something that conveys more information that the average value. The formula works because when we square a number, the result is always a positive value regardless of whether it's a positive or a negative number. By squaring it, then taking the square root, we are assured of getting a positive result

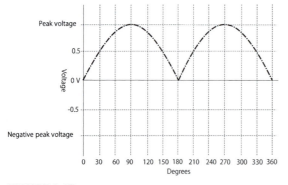

FIGURE 4.17
By squaring the voltage at every point along the sinewave and then taking the square root, we are essentially inverting the negative half cycle.

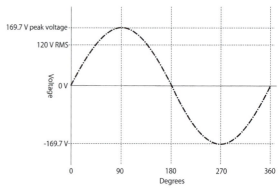

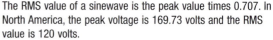

FIGURE 4.18
The RMS value of a sinewave is the peak value times 0.707. In North America, the peak voltage is 169.73 volts and the RMS value is 120 volts.

in the end. In essence, we're inverting the negative half cycle and averaging it with the positive half cycle.

By way of illustration, let's take a sample of a few values in a sinewave and find the RMS value. If we look back at Figure 4.11, we can sample the voltage at 13 points: at 0, 30, 60, 90, 120, 150, 180, 210, 240, 270, 300, and 360°. Then we can plug those values into the equation to solve for the RMS voltage (V_{RMS}):

$$V_{RMS} = \sqrt{\begin{array}{c} [0^2 + .5^2 + .866^2 + 1^2 + .866^2 + .5^2 + 0^2 + (-.5^2) + \\ (-.866^2) + (-.5^2) + 0^2] \div 13 \end{array}}$$

$$V_{RMS} = 0.679$$

If we used more sample points we would get a more accurate answer. Using 37 sample voltages (every 10°) yields an RMS value of 0.70. The more sample points we use, the closer we will get to the number 0.707, which is the actual RMS value for a sinewave with a peak value of 1.

Therefore, to find the RMS value of an AC voltage (assuming it's a pure sinewave), we can simply multiply the peak value, V_{peak}, by 0.707.

$$V_{RMS} = V_{peak} \times 0.707$$

In North America, the standard household power is 120 VAC, which means the peak voltage is (120 ÷ 0.707) = 169.73 VAC.

The RMS value of voltage has much more real-world meaning than the average voltage does. It's the alternating current equivalent of the transfer of DC power. In other words, 120 VAC RMS transfers the same amount of power to a load as would 120 VDC. And remember that power is proportional to the square of the voltage ($P = V^2 \div R$), and the square of a negative number is positive. So even a negative voltage transfers a positive value of power. Another way of thinking about it is that the RMS voltage is equivalent to the DC voltage it would take to produce the same amount of heat in a fixed resistive load. And since the heat produced in a resistor is proportional to the square of the current averaged over a full cycle, that implies that the heat value is proportional to the RMS current.

TRUE RMS METERS

When you are measuring AC voltage, the results you get can vary quite a bit depending on the type of meter you are using. Some meters simply invert the negative half of the waveform and average the results over one cycle, and then apply a weighting factor to approximate the RMS value; this type is a mean reading RMS calibrated meter. Other meters sample the waveform several times during the cycle and perform a calculation over the period to find the true RMS value; this is a true RMS meter. The results of these two operations can be very different, depending on the circumstances.

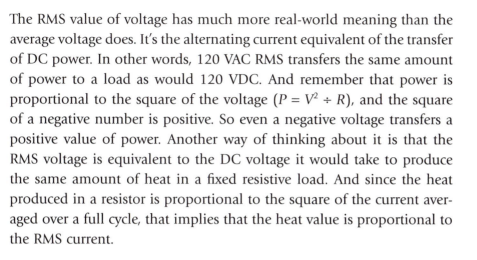

The weighting factor used in a mean reading RMS calibrated meter is based on a pure sinewave. We know that the RMS voltage is 0.707 times the peak voltage in a pure sinewave, and it turns out that the average value of a sinewave in which the negative half cycle has been inverted is 0.636 times the peak value.

Therefore, a mean reading meter "reads" about 0.9 times the RMS value, so by multiplying the output by 1.11 (the inverse of 0.9), it can approximate the RMS value, *but only for a pure sinewave.* This is how a mean reading RMS calibrated meter works.

FIGURE 4.19
A pure voltage sinewave showing the RMS value versus the average value.

49

The problem is that most of the waveforms we encounter today are not pure sinewaves. In dimmers and switch-mode power supplies, also known as electronic power supplies or electronic ballasts, the waveform becomes distorted and it is no longer a pure sinewave. As a result, the weighting factor is no longer accurate and the meter reading can be misleading.

A true RMS meter is the only type of meter that can accurately measure the RMS value of any waveform, even nonsinusoidal waveforms. The meter is limited in accuracy by its frequency response and its dynamic range. A frequency response of about 3000 Hz is usually sufficient, and it should have enough dynamic range to measure a distorted signal in which the ratio between the peak and RMS values is three.

Near the end of the nineteenth century, advances in electrical technology were about to change the world forever. Thomas Edison, following Joseph Swan's blueprint of a carbon filament, platinum wire leads, and a vacuum-enclosed glass bulb, had recently perfected the incandescent lamp, extending its useful life to several hundred hours. The newly established Edison Electric Illuminating Company was feeding on the demand for electric light and power throughout the United States and Europe. As electric streetcars were rapidly replacing horse-drawn trolleys, various metropolitan areas were installing power plants to meet the growing demand for electricity.

FIGURE 4.20
Thomas Edison in his New Jersey lab (c. 1918–1919; courtesy of the National Archives).
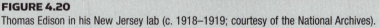

At the time, direct current was the undisputed standard. When Lucien Gaulard and John Dixon Gibbs introduced their new "secondary generator" — known today as a transformer — at the Inventions Exhibition in London, they ignited the imagination of George Westinghouse.* Westinghouse, who had been very successful in the railroad industry, bought the Gaulard-Gibbs patent.

Alternating current was the subject of much debate and speculation, but it suffered from one major drawback: there were no motors that could run on AC power. Therefore, all the advantages of AC power distribution were negated by the lack of its ability to provide locomotion, which was, at the time, one of the major uses of electricity.

DC power distribution, however, was not without drawbacks of its own. There were severe limitations as to how far it could be economically distributed; therefore, power generation had to be decentralized by using small coal-fired "dynamos" generating power for distribution within a half mile (about 800 meters). The dynamos were loud and dirty, and they required the use of an operator. They were generally ill-suited for urban life, which is exactly where they were needed the most. To make matters worse, DC motors were inefficient and required regular maintenance because they used commutators and brushes that wore out. But a DC system of power generation, distribution, lamps, and motors, for all of its shortcomings, was still far superior to gas lamps and manual labor, both of which were a way of life at the time.

In 1884, a young Serbian named Nikola Tesla arrived in New York from his native Europe to go to work for Thomas Edison. He was there by virtue of a recommendation from Edison's associate, Charles Batchelor, who wrote, "My Dear Edison: I know two great men and you are one of them. The other is this young man."

Two years earlier, Tesla had a vision of a polyphase alternating current system that could drive an AC motor. He had worked out the solution mathematically, and he yearned to build a prototype and make it a reality. Eventually, he relayed his idea to Edison, who said in no uncertain terms that he wasn't interested, that it was a waste of time, and that he thought AC was more dangerous than DC.

Despite Edison's rebuff, Tesla continued working for him, hoping that one day he would have a chance to realize his polyphase AC system. Edison offered Tesla a $50,000 bonus — more than $1,000,000 in 2008 dollars — if he improved the efficiency of his DC generators. But when Tesla succeeded in doing so, Edison reneged, saying that his offer was in jest and that Tesla didn't understand American humor.

Shortly afterward, Tesla left the Edison company and with the help of outside investors started his own company to build AC induction motors and generators. The investors eventually took over the company and forced him out because they didn't believe in his approach. Penniless, Tesla resorted to manual labor, digging ditches for a year to

*Empires of Light: Edison, Tesla, Westinghouse, and the Race to Electrify the World, by Jill Jonnes (Random House, 2003).

support himself while searching for another investor. He finally met a financial backer, Charles F. Peck, who he convinced that he had an idea worth pursuing. In 1887 Tesla filed seven patents related to polyphase AC power generation, distribution, and locomotion. He had invented and built an AC motor.

George Westinghouse recognized the value of Tesla's work and bought the patents for about $60,000 (about $1.3M in 2008) in cash and stock in his Westinghouse Corporation, in addition to a royalty of $2.50 for each horsepower of electrical capacity he sold. Tesla and Westinghouse were now partners.

FIGURE 4.21
Nikola Tesla in front of a high-frequency transformer at East Houston Street in New York. (Courtesy of www.teslasociety.com; Dr. Ljubo Vujovic, Secretary General, Tesla Memorial Society of New York.)

But they had much work to do in order to establish the acceptance of this new technology. Alternating current threatened not only Thomas Edison's DC-centric empire, but also the rich and powerful men of Wall Street who provided Edison's financial backing, including J. P. Morgan. Thus, the stage was set for the so-called "War of Currents" between Edison, a staunch proponent of DC, and the team of Tesla and Westinghouse, who had no doubt that AC power distribution was superior. The advantages of AC power distribution were undeniable: it provided a practical means of transmitting electricity efficiently over long distances, allowing the centralization of power generation, and it significantly reduced the cost of electrical transmission by reducing the size of transmission wires. But at that time, it was also unproven.

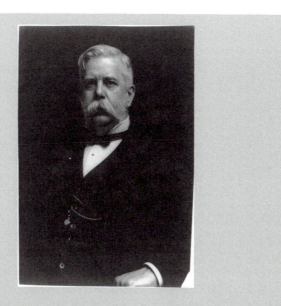

FIGURE 4.22
George Westinghouse, shown here, and Nikola Tesla were allies in the effort to make alternating current the standard for electrical power distribution.

The 1893 Chicago World's Fair was to be the first high-profile battleground for the opposing technologies. Edison and Westinghouse both bid on the job of supplying power to light the fair, but a shortage of copper caused a sharp increase in price. Suddenly, the circumstances dramatically favored the solution with the least use of the metal. Edison's million-dollar bid was halved by Westinghouse, and Westinghouse won the job. In the end, close to 28 million people witnessed the illumination of 93,000 incandescent lamps and 5000 arc lamps, all driven by an AC polyphase power system.

One of the attendees at the Chicago World's Fair was British physicist Lord Kelvin. It just so happened that Kelvin was the head of an international commission to select a design for a soon-to-be-constructed power plant at Niagara Falls. Up until that time, he was a firm believer in DC power distribution. But the demonstration of polyphase AC power distribution at the fair convinced him otherwise. After witnessing the AC power system at the fair, he successfully convinced the commission to award the Niagara Falls contract to Westinghouse. With the reputations of Tesla and Westinghouse riding on the outcome and millions of dollars at stake, the project was successfully completed in 1896. If the world was not yet convinced that AC power distribution was superior, the Niagara Falls project was the final deciding factor. From that point on, the vast majority of electric appliances and equipment was manufactured for AC operation.

That still holds true today. AC allows vast amounts of electricity to be produced in remote locations, transformed to very high voltage, transmitted over very long distances with relatively low current using relatively small conductors, and transformed back to a lower voltage at the point of consumption.

The key to the successful implementation of AC power was the development of the alternating current synchronous motor, which was born in the mind of the young Serbian, Nikola Tesla.

IS AC MORE DEADLY THAN DC?

Near the end of the nineteenth century when Westinghouse was challenging Edison's dominance of commercial power generation and distribution, Edison set out to convince the public that AC was far more dangerous — deadly, even — than DC. He quietly supplied financial support and resources to an electrical engineer and consultant named Harold Brown, who was publicly campaigning for legislation against AC generators and equipment in New York. As part of his campaign, Brown put on public displays designed to demonstrate just how much more dangerous AC was compared to DC. In his first public display, he electrocuted a large black retriever in a lecture hall at Columbia College at 50th and Madison Avenue in New York City, much to the disgust of the members of the audience, which included members of the press, the New York City Board of Electrical Control, and various other interested parties. Many of them walked out in the middle of the demonstration, but Brown persisted until an agent of the American Society for the Prevention of Cruelty to Animals forbade him to electrocute another dog. The demonstration ended, but Brown continued his deadly campaign, successfully electrocuting large dogs, calves, and horses in public.

After one of Brown's demonstrations, a story ran in *The New York Times* describing the grim event. George Westinghouse wrote a letter to the newspaper in response to the article, defending AC. Brown, in turn, wrote a letter to the newspaper challenging Westinghouse to a bizarre contest.

"I challenge Mr. Westinghouse to meet me in the presence of competent electrical experts and take through his body the alternating current while I take through mine a continuous current....We will commence with 100 volts, and will gradually increase the pressure 50 volts at a time, I leading with each increase, until either one or the other has cried enough, and publicly admits his error."*

Westinghouse didn't honor him with a reply.

Is AC really more dangerous than DC? There are many factors that come into play when a person receives a shock. The severity of the shock depends on the size, weight, age, and body fat of the person, as well as voltage, frequency, duration of shock, contact area, contact pressure, temperature, and moisture of the skin. Generally speaking, the impedance of the skin is the first line of defense against a fatal shock. It helps prevent current from flowing through the heart and causing fibrillation. The higher the impedance, the lower the current for a given voltage. Like any other electrical circuit, the flow of current through a human body behaves according to Ohm's law.

It turns out that for AC current, the impedance of our skin decreases as the frequency increases, but the frequencies most likely to cause ventricular fibrillation are between 50 Hz and 60 Hz.

Empires of Light, Jill Jonnes (Random House, 2004).

UNDERSTANDING AC ELECTRICITY

4.1   Why were Tesla's AC patents so important for the widespread acceptance of AC?

4.2   What intrinsic property of atoms produces a magnetic field with a given strength and orientation?

4.3   If everything is made up of atoms, all atoms have electrons, and all electrons have a magnetic dipole, why are some materials more magnetic than others?

4.4   True or false: In some materials, unpaired electrons spontaneously align themselves and reinforce their magnetic fields.

4.5   True or false: The flow of current always produces a magnetic field.

4.6   The right-hand rule is an aid for visualizing the _____ of _____ of a magnetic field around a current-carrying conductor.

4.7   A stationary magnetic field does not induce current in a coil of wire, but a _____ one does.

4.8   What is Faraday's law of induction?

4.9   A wire traveling _____ to the lines of flux in a magnetic field produces no voltage. A wire traveling _____ to the lines of flux in a magnetic field produces maximum voltage.

4.10 A conductor oriented along the Z-axis is traveling at a speed of 3 centimeters per second at an angle of 30° relative to the Y-axis. What is the speed of the conductor in the direction of the X-axis? (Hint: The sine of an angle is the opposite side over the hypotenuse. See the diagram in Figure 4.23.)

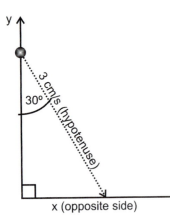

FIGURE 4.23
Z-axis.

4.11 True or false: A conductor moving at a right angle to a magnetic field at a speed of $2x$ inches per second will generate twice the voltage as a conductor moving at a right angle to the same magnetic field at a speed of x inches per second.

4.12 True or false: Fleming's right-hand rule indicates the direction of the force applied to a conductor moving through a magnetic field in a motor.

4.13 What is the sine of 320° rounded to the nearest thousandth? 270°?

4.14 Why are both the sine of zero and the sine of 360° equal to 0?

4.15 If the angle between the direction of travel off a spinning rotor and a magnetic field is 20° and the peak voltage is 169.7 volts, what is the instantaneous voltage?

4.16 What is the voltage of a sinewave at a phase angle of 160° if the peak voltage is 100 volts?

4.17 How fast does a generator have to spin in order to produce a 60-Hz frequency if it has 16 poles?

4.18 If the frequency of a sinewave is 50 Hz, how long does it take to complete one full cycle?

4.19 What is the rotational speed of an eight-pole generator supplying power at 50 Hz?

4.20 In the Excel worksheet created in the exercise on page 42 (Exercise Your Knowledge of Sinewaves), what is the value of the sin at a phase angle of 100°?

4.21 What is the frequency of the mains power in Europe? North America?

4.22 In the exercise on page 42 (Exercise Your Knowledge of Sinewaves), change the formula in cell B1 to "= 169.73*SIN (RADIANS(A1))." Now drag the fill handle (in the lower right-hand corner of cell B1) down to cell B361. Leave the cells highlighted. With the cells still highlighted, click on Insert in the menu, then Chart. This should open the Chart Wizard. In the Chart type, click on Line, and then click Finish. It will

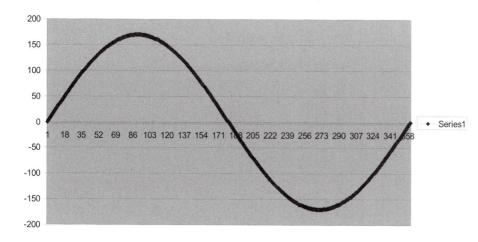

FIGURE 4.24
Sinewave with a peak
value of 169.7 volts.

create a new graph showing a sinewave with a peak value of 169.7 volts, as shown in Figure 4.24.

4.23 If the RMS voltage in Europe is 230 V, what is the peak voltage?

4.24 If we sample a sinewave at 13 evenly spaced points in a single cycle, we get an RMS value of 0.679. But when we average 37 points, we get a value of 0.7. Why does the RMS value of a sinewave change when we used more sample points? How many points would we have to sample to get the answer 0.707?

4.25 A true RMS volt meter is one that calculates the RMS value for any periodic (repeating) waveform. If a voltage is measured with a true RMS meter and also with a voltage averaging meter that inverts the negative half cycle, will the results be the same? Why or why not?

CHAPTER 5
Circuit Elements

"I've never seen electricity; that's why I don't pay for it."

Steven Wright

Our study of electricity and power distribution would be incomplete without understanding certain circuit elements, such as resistors, inductors, capacitors, and transformers, and the way they behave, combine, and interact. Resistance, inductance, and capacitance are elements of impedance; they impede the flow of AC and/or DC. But they do it in different ways. Resistors convert electrical energy to heat energy, while inductors and capacitors store electrical energy. In the process, they each limit the free flow of AC and/or DC.

Resistance is a characteristic that is desirable in some circumstances and undesirable in others. It is desirable when we want to limit the unrestricted flow of current through a circuit and prevent it from destroying the circuit and all of its elements. It is undesirable when we don't want to lose efficiency by the process of converting electrical energy to heat energy. In some cases we take advantage of the electrical-to-heat energy conversion process. Thermal circuit breakers and incandescent lamps would not work without it. In other cases, we try to minimize the effects of the conversion, such as with wire and cable. In large power distribution systems with many circuit elements, the characteristic resistances of each of the elements in the system combine in complex ways. In order to understand how they combine and interact, it's important to understand series and parallel resistance networks.

SERIES RESISTANCE

When two or more resistors are connected in a circuit end to end, they are said to be connected in series.

FIGURE 5.1
A network of resistors in series.

The equivalent resistance of a network of resistors is a single resistor with the same value as the network of resistors. The equivalent resistance of several resistors all connected in series is the sum of the individual resistors.

$$R_{total} = R_1 + R_2 + \cdots + R_{n-1} + R_n,$$

where n = the total number of resistors in series.

Example 5a

Four 100 k-ohm resistors are connected in series. What is their equivalent resistance?

Answer: The total resistance can be calculated by adding the value of each resistor in the series.

FIGURE 5.2

$$R_{total} = 100k + 100k + 100k + 100k$$
$$R_{total} = 400k \text{ ohms}$$

Example 5b

Six resistors with the following values are connected in series: 120 ohms, 150 ohms, 100 ohms, 100 ohms, 250 ohms, and 500 ohms. What is the equivalent resistance?

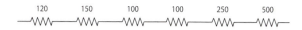

| 120 | 150 | 100 | 100 | 250 | 500 |

FIGURE 5.3

Answer:

$$R_{total} = 120 + 150 + 100 + 100 + 250 + 500$$
$$R_{total} = 1220 \text{ ohms}$$

PARALLEL RESISTANCE

When two or more resistors are all connected across two common nodes, they are said to be connected in parallel.

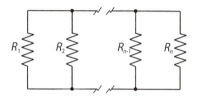

FIGURE 5.4
A network of resistors in parallel.

To find the equivalent resistance of a network of n resistors in parallel, use the following formula:

$$\frac{1}{R_{total}} = \frac{1}{R_1} + \frac{1}{R_2} + \cdots + \frac{1}{R_{n-1}} + \frac{1}{R_n},$$

where R_{total} is the total resistance, R_1 is the first resistor, R_2 is the second resistor, R_{n-1} is the second to last resistor, and R_n is the last resistor.

Example 5c

If four 120 k-ohm resistors are connected in parallel, find the value of the equivalent resistance.

Answer:

$$\frac{1}{R_{total}} = \frac{1}{R_1} + \frac{1}{R_2} + \frac{1}{R_3} + \frac{1}{R_4}$$

$$\frac{1}{R_{total}} = \frac{1}{120k} + \frac{1}{120k} + \frac{1}{120k} + \frac{1}{120k}$$

$$\frac{1}{R_{total}} = \frac{4}{120k}$$

$$R_{total} = \frac{120k}{4}$$

$$R_{total} = 30k = 30,000 \text{ ohms}$$

Example 5d

Six resistors with the following values are connected in parallel: 120 ohms, 150 ohms, 100 ohms, 100 ohms, 250 ohms, 500 ohms. Find the equivalent resistance.

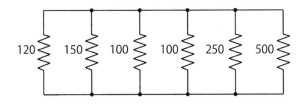

FIGURE 5.5

Answer:

$$\frac{1}{R_{total}} = \frac{1}{R_1} + \frac{1}{R_2} + \frac{1}{R_3} + \frac{1}{R_4} + \frac{1}{R_5} + \frac{1}{R_6}$$

$$\frac{1}{R_{total}} = \frac{1}{120} + \frac{1}{150} + \frac{1}{100} + \frac{1}{100} + \frac{1}{250} + \frac{1}{500}$$

$$\frac{1}{R_{total}} = \frac{25}{3000} + \frac{20}{3000} + \frac{30}{3000} + \frac{30}{3000} + \frac{12}{3000} + \frac{6}{3000}$$

$$\frac{1}{R_{total}} = \frac{123}{3000}$$

$$R_{total} = \frac{3000}{123}$$

$$R_{total} = 24.39 \text{ ohms}$$

SERIES/PARALLEL RESISTANCE

If a circuit has resistors connected both in series and in parallel, the equivalent resistance can be found by calculating the equivalent value of the parallel and series resistors individually, and then combining them.

Example 5e

Find the total value of resistance in Figure 5.6 below:

Answer:

Step 1: Calculate the value of the parallel resistor network. From the previous example, we know the total resistance is 24.39 ohms.

Step 2: Replace the parallel resistor network with a single resistor of the same value and redraw the network as in Figure 5.7.

Step 3: Sum the series resistors: R_{total} = 100 + 24.39 + 100 = 224.39 ohms.

63

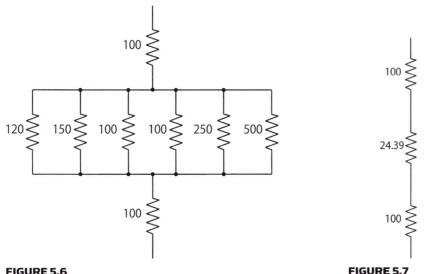

FIGURE 5.6   **FIGURE 5.7**

REAL-WORLD RESISTANCE

In the real world there is no such thing as a perfect conductor; every component in a circuit or system has some value of resistance, however small. Sometimes we intentionally place resistors in a circuit in order to achieve an objective, such as when we use a data terminator to match the impedance of a cable. Other times we would rather have a complete lack of resistance, such as in a power distribution system where resistance contributes to the inefficiency of the system. Resistance that is not intentionally designed into a system is parasitic resistance.

Parasitic resistance can be found in feeder cable, connectors, across the junctions of electronic switches and devices, in the windings of a motor or transformer, even in the interface between a plug and receptacle. Sometimes it is so small that it can be ignored in practice, and other times it must be carefully considered and compensated for. For example, a 4/0 (pronounced "four ought") feeder cable has a relatively low characteristic resistance of 0.049 ohms per 1000 feet, primarily because of its large diameter. If we run a short length of it, say 25 feet, from a feeder transformer or company switch to a power distribution panel, then the total resistance is 0.001225 ohms. The voltage drop produced by the parasitic resistance when the current is 400 amps is 0.49 volts. (Remember Ohm's law? The voltage drop is the resistance times the current.) It's a negligible voltage drop, although it represents 196 watts lost to heat (I^2 losses).

On the other hand, if we're running a branch circuit with #12 AWG (American Wire Gage) wire, it has a much smaller diameter and therefore a higher characteristic resistance. If we have a run of 300 feet, then we have to pay attention to the voltage drop caused by the resistance of the length of wire.

Example 5f

#12 AWG wire has a characteristic resistance of 5.20864 ohms per kilometer. What is the resistance of a 100-meter run?

Answer: 5.20864 ohms per 1000 meters is the same as 0.00520864 ohms per meter. Therefore, to find the total resistance of a length of wire, we can multiply that number by the number of meters in the run.

Resistance (ohms) = 0.00520864 ohms per meter × 100 meters = 0.520864 ohms

IMPEDANCE

When we're dealing with direct current, the only impediment to the flow of current is resistance. But with alternating current there are other elements in addition to resistance that interact with the current and affect how the circuit behaves. Reactance is also a measure of the electrical opposition to the flow of alternating current. It comes from the behavior of inductors and capacitors and how they affect the flow current due to the effects of magnetism and/or electrical charges. The combination of DC resistance and AC reactance is called impedance.

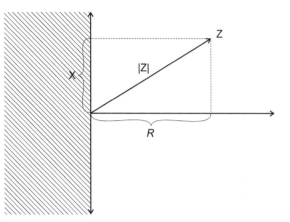

FIGURE 5.8
Impedance Z is the combination of resistance R and reactance X. Note that resistance can only be a positive value but reactance can be positive or negative.

65

REACTANCE

Reactance is an element of impedance that stems from the magnetism or stored charge in an AC circuit. The ratio of the magnetic flux to the amount of current is called inductance, and the ratio of the stored charge to the voltage in a circuit is called capacitance. If the reactance in a circuit is more inductive than capacitive, then it is an inductive reactance; if the reactance is more capacitive than inductive, then it is a capacitive reactance. How a circuit or circuit element becomes inductive or capacitive is a matter of its physical characteristics. Stray inductance and capacitance, much like parasitic resistance, is almost always present to some degree in a circuit, and sometimes we purposefully build and insert inductors or capacitors in a circuit for various reasons. To better understand inductive and capacitive reactance, we need to know more about inductors and capacitors.

INDUCTORS

To build an inductor, we would take a length of wire and wrap it around a cylinder, like a coil. If we connect this inductor to a DC power supply, then the flow of current through the wire will set up a strong magnetic

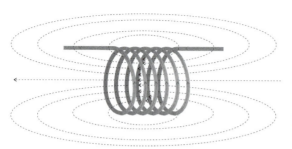

FIGURE 5.9
Cross sectional view of the magnetic field around an inductor.
Note that an inductor does not impede the flow of DC current.

FIGURE 5.10
An inductor wound on a toroidal iron core. (Photo courtesy of
Leviton.)

field through the center of the coil. (Remember the right-hand rule?)
Each turn in the coil reinforces and strengthens the magnetic field. To DC,
an inductor — remember, it's simply a coil of wire — is a direct short. It
has no impedance other than the characteristic resistance of the wire.

But if we connect the inductor to an AC source, something very interest-
ing happens. During the positive half cycle, the current sets up a strong
magnetic field in one direction. When the current reverses direction
during the negative half cycle, the magnetic field that was set up by the
positive half cycle does not collapse right away; it takes time. During
the time that the magnetic field is collapsing, it is in direct opposition
to the magnetic field that is trying to set up due to the negative half cycle
of current. Therefore, the inductor opposes the change of current, provid-
ing an impediment to the free flow of current. It acts as a "choke." After
a short while, the magnetic field collapses completely and the current
flowing in the opposite direction sets up the magnetic field again, but
in the opposite orientation. Both the current and the magnetic field are
constantly changing directions, and the current is constantly impeded.

In our water–electricity analogy, an inductor may be thought of as a large
paddle wheel or a turbine blade in a channel of water. When the water
flows, it starts the paddle wheel turning, giving it momentum. If the
water current suddenly changes direction, the paddle wheel will resist it
because it's turning the other way. Once the reverse current overcomes

the momentum of the wheel it will begin to turn the other way. But it initially resists the change in direction until the momentum is overcome. The same is true of an electrical current. The magnetic field of the inductor is like the momentum in the paddle wheel.

FIGURE 5.11
Inductor symbols with and without an iron core.

Inductance is measured in henrys, after the American scientist Joseph Henry. But it is often represented in mathematic equations by the letter "L," after Heinrich Lenz, a Baltic German physicist who advanced the study of inductance. The henry is a very large value; therefore, it is more common for inductors to be measured in millihenries (10^{-3} henrys or 0.001 henrys).

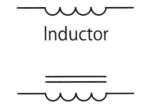

In a vacuum, the value of an inductor depends on the diameter of the wire or the wire gauge, the diameter of the coil, and the number of turns in the coil. By inserting an iron core in the center of an inductor, the inductance increases in direct proportion to the permeability of the iron core, i.e., the more the magnetic field influences the core material, the higher the inductance.

67

$$\text{Inductance }(L) \sim \left[(\text{Number of turns})^2 \times (\text{Area of wire cross section})\right] \div \text{length of coil}$$

Inductance is a measure of the inherent value of an inductor but it is not an absolute measure of the impedance to the flow of current because the impedance is frequency dependent. As we said earlier, an inductor offers no impedance to the flow of DC (other than the small resistance of the wire), but it does impede the flow of AC. As the frequency of the alternating current in an inductor increases, so does the impedance. The amount of impedance in an inductor is called inductive reactance, X_L, and it is measured in ohms.

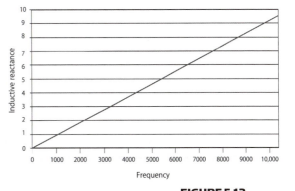

FIGURE 5.12
As the frequency increases, so does the inductive reactance in an inductor.

$$X_L(\text{ohms}) = 2\pi f L,$$

where X_L is the inductive reactance, π is pi (3.14), f is the frequency in hertz, and L is the inductance in henrys.

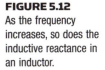

Example 5g

What is the inductive reactance of a load with an inductance of 500 millihenries at a frequency of 50 Hz?

Answer:

$$X_L = 2\pi f L$$

$$X_L = 2 \times \pi \times 50 \times 0.500$$

$$X_L = 157 \text{ ohms}$$

Reactance is to AC what resistance is to DC. Ohm's law describes the relationship between the voltage, current, and reactance in an AC circuit just as it describes the relationship between voltage, current, and resistance in a DC circuit.

Example 5h

If the inductor above (500 millihenries) is connected to a 230 V power supply at 50 Hz, how much current would flow through it?

Answer:

$$V = I \times X_L$$

$$230 = I \times 157$$

$$I = 230 \div 157 = 1.46 \text{A}$$

In electronic circuits, inductors are often built in for specific purposes: to tune a circuit to a particular frequency, to filter out certain frequencies, etc. But in a typical power distribution system, inductance is often an unintentional by-product of the physical layout. Many components in a typical entertainment production system have some natural inductance, for example, motors, transformers, ballasts, and even lamp filaments, to a small degree. As we will see later on, inductance introduces a shift between the waveforms of the voltage and current, which has many important consequences in a power distribution system.

CAPACITORS

A capacitor is a device that can temporarily store an electrostatic charge in an electric field between two plates separated by an insulating mate-

rial. It collects negatively charged electrons on one plate and positively charged holes on the other, each having a charge of equal magnitude but opposite polarity. A capacitor is similar to a temporary battery except that a battery produces a charge through a chemical reaction while a capacitor can only obtain a charge from an external source.

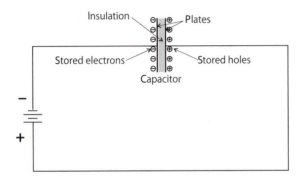

FIGURE 5.13
A capacitor stores a charge by collecting negatively charged electrons and positively charged holes on two plates separated by an insulating material.

69

In our water–electricity analogy, a capacitor can be thought of as a water tower that temporarily stores water from a reservoir until it is needed. It cannot generate new water; it can only take on water that is pumped from the reservoir. It holds the water at elevation so that the water pressure assures delivery on demand.

The value of a capacitor is measured in farads, after Michael Faraday, a British physicist and chemist who discovered electromagnetic induction. A farad is a very large quantity, so most capacitors have a value in microfarads (0.000001 farads or 10^{-6} farads) or smaller.

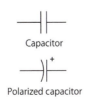

FIGURE 5.14
Symbols for a capacitor (top) and a polarized capacitor.

FIGURE 5.15
A capacitor in an automated luminaire.

The classic capacitor is a discrete component made from two layers of foil separated by an insulating polymer film, mica, or paper. The foil collects the charges when a voltage is applied to the two leads, and it discharges when it finds a path for the flow of electrons.

Because the two plates in a capacitor are separated by an insulating material, a capacitor acts like an open circuit to a DC source once it is charged. In an AC circuit, however, a capacitor resists the flow of current because of the stored charge opposes the applied voltage. The resistance to the flow of current in a capacitor is called capacitive reactance, X_C, and it is measured in ohms.

$$X_C = \frac{1}{2\pi fC},$$

where X_C is the capacitive reactance, f is the frequency, and C is the capacitance in farads.

70

Example 5i

What is the capacitive reactance of a load with a capacitance of 250 microfarads at 150 kHz?

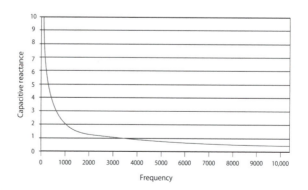

FIGURE 5.16
Capacitive reactance versus frequency; the higher the frequency, the lower the capacitive reactance. Notice that the capacitive reactance is infinite — or an open circuit — at 0 Hz (which is DC).

Answer:

$$X_C = \frac{1}{2\pi fC}$$

$$X_C = \frac{1}{2 \times \pi \times 150{,}000 \times 0.00025}$$

$$X_C = \frac{1}{235.5}$$

$$X_C = 0.00425 \text{ ohms}$$

PHASE ANGLES

In a purely resistive load, current flows instantaneously when voltage is applied to a circuit. In an inductor, however, there is a lag between the time that the voltage is applied and the time the current starts flowing. The current lags behind the voltage because all of the energy flowing to the inductor initially goes into setting up a magnetic field before it starts pushing electrons through the circuit.

In a capacitor, there is also a lag time, but in this case it's the voltage that lags behind the current. That's because the capacitor has to first build a charge from zero volts to the applied voltage.

In each case, the lag between the voltage and current is called the phase angle because it can be measured by the angle in degrees between the start of the voltage and the start of the current. The amount of lag time depends on how much resistance, inductance, or capacitance is in the circuit. For example, if, in a partially inductive and partially resistive load, the applied voltage leads the current by an eighth of a cycle, then the phase angle is 45° because one-eighth of 360° is 45°. But a purely resistive load has no lag time; in a purely inductive load the voltage leads the current by 90°, and in a purely capacitive load the current leads the voltage by 90°.

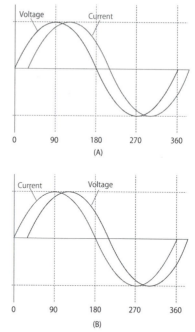

FIGURE 5.17
Top: Voltage leading current. Bottom: Current leading voltage.

The phase relationships between the voltage and current in an inductor and a capacitor can be more easily remembered with the help of the phrase "ELI the ICEman." ELI is a mnemonic for the voltage (or EMF) leading the current (I) in an inductor (L). ICE is a mnemonic for the current (I) leading the voltage (EMF) in a capacitor (C).

COMPLEX IMPEDANCE

In real life, there is no such thing as a purely resistive load. Every load has some element of resistance and some element of inductance or capacitance. For example, loads with windings, like motors and transformers, are highly inductive. Even a pair of long conductors, like feeder cables or a branch circuit, could exhibit stray capacitance or mutual inductance. In addition, the resistance of the wire adds a resistive element, however small.

The combination of resistance, capacitive reactance, and inductive reactance make up the impedance of a load. But impedance is a complex number, meaning it has both a magnitude and a direction (or phase angle). By the same token, inductance and capacitance are also complex numbers; they also have both a magnitude and a phase angle. Because they are complex numbers, they can be represented in vector form where the length of the vector represents the magnitude and the direction represents the phase angle. Since resistors always have a phase angle of zero, we can show a graphical representation of complex impedance in a plane where the resistance is shown along the X-axis and the reactance is shown along the Y-axis.

Notice that the resistance can only be a positive number, while reactance can be either positive or negative. A positive reactance indicates that the impedance is more inductive than it is capacitive, and a negative reactance indicates that the impedance is more capacitive than inductive.

We can calculate the magnitude of the impedance if we know the value of the resistance and the magnitude of the reactance by using the Pythagorean theorem. The letter Z is often used to represent impedance.

$$\text{Impedance}^2 \, (\text{ohms}) = \text{Resistance}^2 \, (\text{ohms}) + \text{Reactance}^2 \, (\text{ohms}),$$

where reactance = $X_L - X_C$, or

$$Z^2 = R^2 + (X_L - X_C)^2.$$

The complete value of impedance includes both a magnitude and a phase. If a load is more inductive than capacitive, then the current will lag behind the voltage in that load. If the load is more capacitive than inductive, then the voltage will lag behind the current.

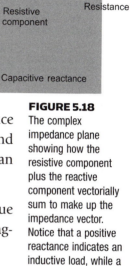

FIGURE 5.18
The complex impedance plane showing how the resistive component plus the reactive component vectorially sum to make up the impedance vector. Notice that a positive reactance indicates an inductive load, while a negative reactance indicates a capacitive load.

73

Example 5j

In the 60-Hz circuit shown in Figure 5.19, the load has a resistance of 75 ohms, an inductance of 75 millihenries, and a capacitance of 25 microfarads. What is the magnitude of the impedance?

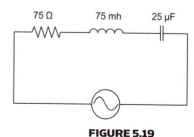

FIGURE 5.19

Answer:

Step 1: First, calculate the inductive reactance and the capacitive reactance.

$$X_L = 2\pi fL$$

$$X_L = 2 \times \pi \times 60 \times 0.075$$

$$X_L = 28.26 \text{ ohms}$$

$$X_C = \frac{1}{2\pi fC}$$

$$X_C = \frac{1}{2 \times \pi \times 60 \times 0.000025}$$

$$X_C = \frac{1}{.00942}$$

$$X_C = 106.1 \text{ ohms}$$

Step 2: Calculate the impedance.

$$Z^2 = R^2 + (X_L - X_C)^2$$

$$Z^2 = 75^2 + (28.26 - 106.12)^2$$

$$Z^2 = 5.625 \times 10^3 + (-77.9)^2$$

$$Z^2 = 5.625 \times 10^3 + 6067.96$$

$$Z = \sqrt{11692.96}$$

$$Z = 108.13 \text{ ohms}$$

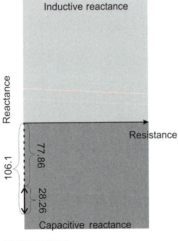

FIGURE 5.20

Example 5k

Calculate the phase angle in the above example.

Answer:

Step 1: Sum the vectors of the inductive reactance and the capacitive reactance as shown in Figure 5.20.

Reactance $= 106.12 - 28.26$ ohms $= 77.86$ ohms

Since the magnitude of the capacitive reactance is larger than the magnitude of the inductive reactance, the sum is more capacitive.

Step 2: Vectorially sum the capacitive reactance and the resistance as shown in Figure 5.21.

Now that we can see the relationship between the phase angle, the capacitive reactance, and the resistance, as shown in Figure 5.21, we can use the formula for tangents to calculate the phase angle.

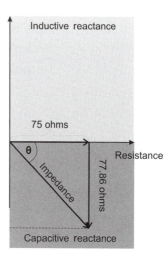

FIGURE 5.21

$$\tan\theta = \text{opposite side} \div \text{adjacent side} = 77.86 \div 75$$

$$\theta = \arctan(1.038)$$

$$\theta = 46°$$

TRANSFORMERS

Transformers play a very important role in the distribution of alternating current electricity. They were instrumental in the widespread acceptance of AC power distribution at the turn of the twentieth century when Tesla and Westinghouse were challenging Edison's dominance with DC systems. The AC distribution model ultimately won out because it is more economical and practical than DC power distribution, and transformers have a lot to do with it.

A transformer converts voltage from high to low, or vice versa, while maintaining the power transferred (with the exception of losses due to inefficiency). This allows large quantities of energy to be transported over long distances at relatively low currents, significantly reducing I^2R losses and saving money on copper, labor, and materials. It also allows systems to be designed to deliver electricity at relatively low voltages, which makes it safer to use.

A transformer is built by winding two coils around an iron core, usually sharing a common frame. The windings are close enough to each other that they become inductively coupled or linked through the magnetic field that is generated when one winding is energized by the flow of current. The winding that is connected to the voltage source is the primary and the side that is connected to the load is the secondary.

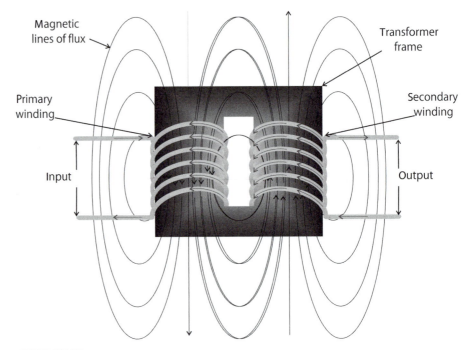

Magnetic lines of flux

Transformer frame

Primary winding

Secondary winding

Input

Output

FIGURE 5.22
A transformer showing the primary and secondary windings wrapped around two cores sharing a common frame.

When AC current flows through the primary winding, the magnetic field around it increases as the current increases. As the magnetic field grows, the lines of flux cut the windings of the secondary coil, thus inducing a secondary current. The strength of the magnetic field in the primary winding depends on the number of turns, and the voltage in the secondary depends on the ratio of the number of turns in the primary to the number of turns in the secondary, as well as the input voltage on the primary. If the voltage is increased from the primary to the secondary, it's a step-up transformer, and if the voltage is decreased, it's a step-down transformer.

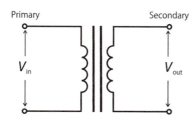

Primary　　　　　　　　　　Secondary

V_{in}　　　　　　　　　　　V_{out}

$V_p/V_s = N_p/N_s$

FIGURE 5.23
Transformer symbol. The ratio of the input (primary) voltage to the output (secondary) voltage is the same as the ratio of the number of turns in the primary to the number of turns in the secondary.

The ratio of number of turns in the primary to the number of turns in the secondary is called the turns ratio. The output voltage is the product of the input voltage and the turns ratio.

$$V_{out} = V_{in} \times \frac{turns\,(secondary)}{turns\,(primary)}$$

Example 5l

A 120/240 V transformer has 50 turns in the primary. How many turns does the secondary winding have?

Answer: 100.

Example 5m

A transformer has a turns ratio of $8:115$ (primary to secondary). What should the input voltage be in order to generate 6900 volts at the output?

Answer:

$$V_{sec} = V_{pri} \times \frac{turns\,(secondary)}{turns\,(primary)}$$

$$6900 = V_{pri} \times \frac{115}{8}$$

$$V_{pri} = 6900 \times 8 \div 115 = 480 \text{ volts.}$$

77

Transformers come in a wide range of sizes and styles, from a small transformer that will step down the voltage from 120 or 240 volts to 12 or 24 volts to very large feeder transformers that distribute power to metropolitan areas. Transformers are rated according to the amount of power that they can safely handle and they are usually rated in volt-amps or kilovolt-amps.

UNDERSTANDING CIRCUIT ELEMENTS

5.1   What is the equivalent resistance of the resistor networks shown below?

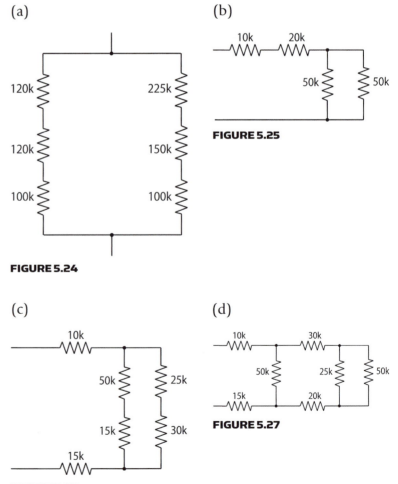

(a)

FIGURE 5.24

(b)

FIGURE 5.25

(c)

FIGURE 5.26

(d)

FIGURE 5.27

5.2 Find the total value of resistance in the following circuit:

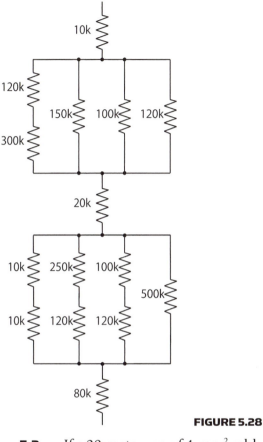

FIGURE 5.28

5.3 If a 20-meter run of 4-mm² cable has a characteristic resistance of 0.011 ohms per meter, how much current would produce a 6.6-volt drop?

5.4 What is the longest length of 1.5-mm² cable, which has a characteristic resistance of 0.029 ohms per meter, that can be run if the maximum allowable voltage drop is 9.2 volts and the current is 16 amps?

5.5 What is the voltage drop across a 40-meter length of 6-mm² cable carrying 45 amps if the characteristic resistance of the cable is 0.0073 ohms per meter?

5.6 If #12 AWG wire is run 250 feet to the load and another 250 feet from the load back to the power distribution panel, what is the total resistance of the entire circuit? The characteristic resistance of #12 AWG is 5.20864 ohms per 1000 meters.

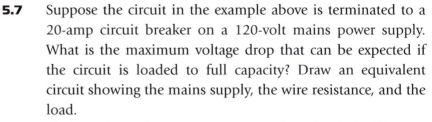

5.7   Suppose the circuit in the example above is terminated to a 20-amp circuit breaker on a 120-volt mains power supply. What is the maximum voltage drop that can be expected if the circuit is loaded to full capacity? Draw an equivalent circuit showing the mains supply, the wire resistance, and the load.

5.8   If a lamp is rated 1000 watts at 120 volts, what is the filament resistance at that voltage? Draw an equivalent circuit showing the lamp connected to a circuit breaker and a 350-foot run of 2-conductor #12 AWG (350 feet to the load and 350 feet back to the panel).

5.9   In the example above, if the mains supply was 120 volts, what is the applied voltage at the lamp? (Assume that the resistance of the filament is independent of the voltage and current even though in real life it's not.)

5.10   Suppose that you have a 15-amp, 230VAC service and you want to deliver power to the load with a maximum voltage drop of 4%. If you use 1.5-mm cable, which has a characteristic resistance of 0.029 ohms per meter, what is the maximum allowable length of a run?

5.11   Impedance is the combination of _____ and _____.

5.12   The ratio of magnetic flux to current is called _____.

5.13   The ratio of _____ _____ to current is called capacitance.

5.14   Describe why an inductor opposes the flow of AC.

5.15   What is the inductive reactance of a load with an inductance of 250 millihenries at a frequency of 60 Hz?

5.16   If a 750-millihenry inductor is connected to a 120 V power supply at 60 Hz, how much current would flow through it?

5.17   To DC, a capacitor acts as an _____ _____.

5.18   What is the capacitive reactance of a load with a 750-microfarad capacitor if the frequency is 50 Hz?

5.19   In an inductor, the _____ leads the _____.

5.20   A complex number is one that has both a _____ and a _____.

5.21   In a 60-Hz circuit, a load has a resistance of 150 ohms, an inductance of 150 millihenries, and a capacitance of 250 microfarads. What is the magnitude of the impedance?

5.22   What is the phase angle of the impedance in 5.21 above?

5.23   If a 480/240 V transformer has 200 turns in the primary, how many turns does the secondary winding have?

5.24   If a transformer has a turns ratio of 10:130 (primary to secondary), what should the input voltage be in order to generate 13,000 volts at the output?

5.25   If the turns ratio of a transformer is greater than one, is it a step-up or a step-down transformer?

CHAPTER 6

AC Power

"One afternoon, which is ever present in my recollection, I was enjoying a walk with my friend in the city park and reciting poetry. At that age I knew entire books by heart, word for word. One of these was Goethe's Faust. The sun was just setting and reminded me of a glorious passage:

'The glow retreats, done is the day of toil;
It yonder hastes, new fields of life exploring;
Ah, that no wing can lift me from the soil
Upon its track to follow, follow soaring!'

As I uttered these inspiring words the idea came like a flash of lightning and in an instant the truth was revealed. I drew with a stick on the sand the diagram shown six years later in my address before the American Institute of Electrical Engineers, and my companion understood them perfectly. The images I saw were wonderfully sharp and clear and had the solidity of metal and stone, so much so that I told him, 'See my motor here; watch me reverse it.' I cannot begin to describe my emotions. Pygmalion seeing his statue come to life could not have been more deeply moved."

Nikola Tesla, as quoted in *The Autobiography of Nikola Tesla*

Electrical power is not a difficult concept to grasp, but there are some subtle and some not-so-subtle nuances. For example, the difference between DC power and AC power is slight, but important. In a DC system, power is simply the product of the voltage and the current.

$$\text{DC power (watts)} = \text{Voltage (volts)} \times \text{Current (amps)}$$

In an AC system, the power at any instant in time (the instantaneous power) is also the product of the voltage and the current. But since the voltage and current may or may not be in phase, the average power over a full cycle can vary quite a bit. If the voltage and current are in phase with each other (phase angle = 0°), then the average power is the RMS voltage times the RMS current (and the peak power is the peak voltage times the peak current). On the other hand, if the voltage and current are 90° out of phase with each other (phase angle = 90°, as in a pure inductor), then the real power used is zero.

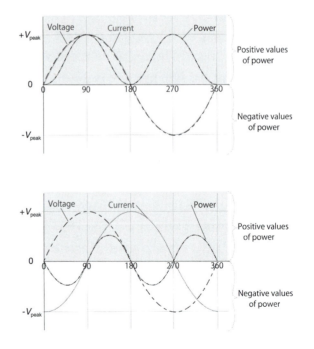

FIGURE 6.1
(Top) Multiplying two sinewaves in phase with each other produce a positive result; (bottom) multiplying two sinewaves 90° out of phase with each other produces a result that averages zero.

The key to the difference is the phase angle. When we multiply two sinewaves in phase with each other we get a third sinewave of twice the frequency, and it lies entirely in the positive quadrant of the X–Y plane. But when we multiply two sinewaves that are 90° out of phase with each we get a third sinewave of twice the frequency, half of which is in the positive quadrant and half of which is in the negative quadrant. Its average over the entire cycle is zero.

AC POWER FORMULA

When the phase angle is between zero and 90°, the average power varies between 100% and zero percent. In fact, the exact percentage is a function of the cosine of the phase angle. For example, if the phase angle is 45°, then the power is reduced to 70.71% of maximum because the cosine of 45° is 0.7071 (to convert a decimal to percentage, multiply by 100). We can modify the DC power formula for AC by factoring in the cosine of the phase angle, as shown below:

$$\text{AC power (watts)} = \text{Voltage (volts)} \times \text{Current (amps)} \times \cos\theta$$

POWER FACTOR

We can verify that when the voltage and current are in phase with each other, the phase angle is 0° and the cosine of 0° is 1; therefore, the multiplying factor (or the cosine of θ) is 1. But when the voltage and current are 90° out of phase with each other, since the cosine of 90° is 0, the multiplying factor is 0 and the resulting power is 0 watts.

This multiplying factor, the cosine of the phase angle, is called the power factor. Ultimately, we end up with the following formula for AC power:

$$\text{AC power (watts)} = \text{Voltage (volts)} \times \text{Current (amps)} \times \text{Power factor,}$$

where the power factor is the cosine of the phase angle.

Notice that the value of the power factor scales the consumed power by a factor from 0 to 1, depending on the phase angle, but the current doesn't change. Another way of looking at it is that, for a given amount

85

of consumed power, the current goes up as the phase angle gets closer to 90°.

Power factor is a very important concept in power distribution. If the power factor is a very small number, then little power is being consumed even though the current flowing through the system is very large. That's because the voltage and current are so far out of phase that little work is being done. Distributing power in this manner requires much more current-handling capability than is really necessary. Everything in the system has to be oversized to deliver the same amount of power—the generator, power distribution cables, transmission towers, switches, transformers, breakers, and connectors all have to be oversized to handle the increase in current. In addition, the labor to install the larger system, including hundreds of miles of cables and distribution gear, adds to the inflated cost.

On the component level, an automated lighting fixture with a low power factor, for example, requires more current to produce the same amount of light. It also requires bigger fuses, breakers, internal wiring, transformers, switches and power supplies, all of which add to the size, weight, and cost of the fixture.

Utility companies that sell electricity hate to supply electricity to customers with highly reactive loads with a low power factor. It places a high demand on their delivery system and strains their resources. It costs them millions of dollars to bring more supply online.

POWER FACTOR CORRECTION

It's easy to see why the power factor is very important and why it's desirable to keep it as high as possible. Loads like transformers, heating elements, filaments, motors, and ballasts are inductive and are sometimes power factor–corrected by adding capacitors to the circuit. Adding capacitance to an inductive load changes the phase relationship and brings the voltage and current back in phase if the capacitive reactance exactly balances the inductive reactance. Many automated lighting fixtures have a power factor correction capacitor. You may also see banks of large, oil-filled capacitors on transmission towers or in electrical substations, particularly in industrial areas like refineries that consume lots of power, for the same reason.

Because of the increased costs associated with delivering power to loads with a low power factor, power companies normally build in a demand component in their billing to incentivize consumers of electricity, particularly large consumers, to keep their overall power factor as high as possible. That helps them keep their costs lower by minimizing the current they have to deliver in order to supply a given amount of power.

COMPLEX POWER

You may wonder what happens to the energy when a low power factor causes a large current to flow but little power to be consumed. After all, the flow of current requires energy, and if it's not being consumed by the load, then it must be going somewhere.

It turns out that when the phase angle between the voltage and the current is large, then the energy flows back and forth between the source and the load. The mechanism for the energy transfer is the temporary storage of energy in the magnetic or electrostatic field of the reactive load. For example, if the load is purely capacitive, then the current flowing to the load is temporarily stored in the form of energy by the capacitor's electrostatic field. That energy is subsequently returned to the source (minus the losses due to inefficiency) when the current changes direction and the electrostatic field discharges. The result is that the net power transferred is zero.

In the case of a purely capacitive or a purely inductive load, the power that is shuttled back and forth between the source and the load is reactive power. It does no work, and is therefore sometimes referred to as wattless power. The power that is consumed by the load is called real power. Reactive power and real power have both a magnitude and a phase. The phase of real power is always 0° (the voltage and current are always in phase), and the phase of reactive power is always 90° for inductive loads and –90° for capacitive loads. The vector sum of real power and reactive power is complex power.

87

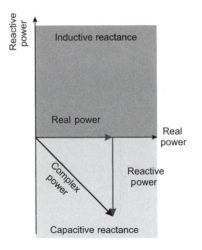

FIGURE 6.2
Complex power is the vector sum of the real power and reactive power. Notice that the phase angle of real power is always 0° and the phase angle of the reactive power is always 90° (inductive loads) or −90° (capacitive loads).

The magnitude of the complex power is often referred to as apparent power, because its value is the product of the voltage and current — the power that, if we know nothing else about the load, is apparently being consumed. The units of measure for apparent power are volt-amps (VA) or kilovolt-amps (kVA). Reactive power is sometimes referred to as VARs, for volts-amps-reactive. Large motors sometimes have a kVAR rating on the nameplate. The relationship between the magnitude of the real power, reactive power, and complex power is shown below:

$$|\text{Apparent power}| = \sqrt{(\text{Real power}^2 + \text{Reactive power}^2)}$$

One of the main reasons that complex power is of interest to us as production electricians or electrical engineers is that we need to know how to size our power distro correctly in order to handle the current flow. Some of that current flow is due to real power and some is due to reactive power, and if we are unaware of the reactive power component in a reactive load, then we will undersize our power distribution system.

Example 6a

Suppose we measure 230 VAC and 10.5 amps in a circuit. What is the apparent power?

Answer: 2415 watts.

Example 6b

If the nameplate on the load in the above example tells us that the power factor is 0.8, then what is the phase angle? What is the real power? What is the reactive power?

Answer:

$$\text{Phase angle} = \text{Inverse}(\cos 0.8) = 36.9°$$

$$\text{Real power (watts)} = 230 \text{ volts} \times 10.5 \text{ amps} \times 0.8$$

$$\text{Real power (watts)} = 1932 \text{ watts}$$

$$\text{Reactive power} = \sqrt{(\text{Apparent power}^2 - \text{Real power}^2)}$$

$$\text{Reactive power} = \sqrt{(2415^2 - 1932^2)} = 1449 \text{ watts}$$

89

THREE-PHASE POWER

Westinghouse and Tesla were very influential in the use of multiphase power distribution. It offers versatility in the way it is connected and the voltage it delivers, it requires less copper to transmit the same amount of power as a single-phase system, and it is ideal for powering motors because each of the phases peak at different times, delivering evenly distributed torque. The vast majority of power that is generated for commercial applications throughout the world today is distributed using multiphase transmission, and much of that is three-phase power.

A single-phase, two-pole generator either has a stator with a bi-polar magnet and a rotor with a pair of windings connected in parallel (with opposing polarity so that the voltages reinforce each other rather than cancel), or it has a stator with two windings connected in parallel and a rotor with a bi-polar magnet. Either way, it has only one pair of

windings and one bi-polar magnet. If we added two more sets of windings, each set connected in parallel, and oriented them so that they were spaced 120° apart from each other, then each of the winding pairs would generate their own voltage sinewave as the magnetic poles rotate. The result would be a three-phase power system.

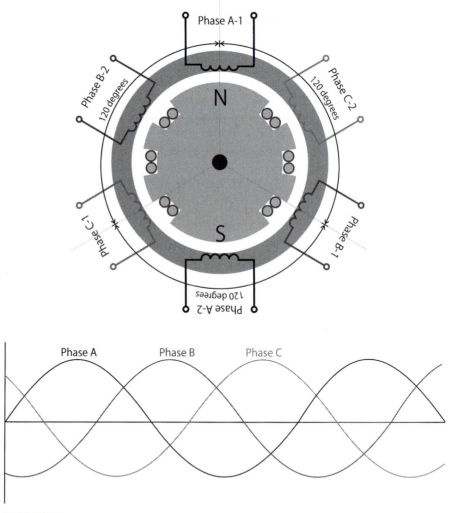

FIGURE 6.3
A two-pole, three-phase generator showing three pairs of windings spaced 120° apart from each other. Each pair of windings is connected in parallel and opposite in polarity so that the voltages reinforce each other.

Not all generators have only two poles; some have as many as 18 or more. In a synchronous generator, the mechanical speed or rotation is inversely proportional to the number of poles. Two-pole synchronous generators producing 50 or 60 Hz rotate at 3000 or 3600 RPM, respectively. This type of generator is typically used with coal-fired steam turbine generators because the steam turbine rotates at a high rate of speed. Nuclear steam turbine generators generally require lower shaft speeds and often use four-pole generators spinning at 1500 or 1800 RPM. Diesel-powered portable generators cannot rotate at high rates of speed, so they typically have a large number of poles.

THREE-PHASE POWER CALCULATIONS

In this chapter we introduced the power factor and learned that we have to use the cosine of the phase angle in the AC power equation. That takes into account the phase angle between the voltage and the current for single-phase power calculations.

When we're dealing with three-phase power, there is another factor that must be taken into consideration and that adds another dimension to the power equation. Since each of the three phases are 120° apart from each other, they interact differently than we might expect. When they share a common conductor, as they often do, the currents do not sum in a straightforward way; they add vectorially.

For example, if phase A and phase B have a common node, then any conductor connected to that node will carry the current from phase A and phase B. But since they are 120° apart from each other, we have to add them vectorially to find the resulting current through that conductor.

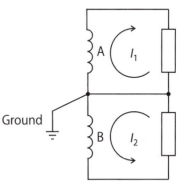

If we look at the illustration to the right, we can see that the current going through the common conductor is the vectorial sum of I_1 and I_2.

$$\overrightarrow{I_{total}} = \overrightarrow{I_1} + \overrightarrow{I_2}$$

Since we know the phase angle is 120°, we can show a graphical representation of the vectorial sum, as in Figure 6.5.

FIGURE 6.4
In a three-phase power system, when any two phases share a common node, the current flowing through the common conductor adds vectorially.

91

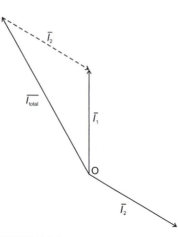

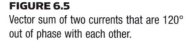

FIGURE 6.5
Vector sum of two currents that are 120°
out of phase with each other.

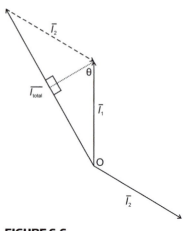

FIGURE 6.6
By drawing a perpendicular line from the
end of I_1 to I_{total}, we can break the triangle
into two right triangles. This will help us
find the magnitude of I_{total}.

For the sake of simplicity we'll take the case where I_1 and I_2 are equal in
magnitude. We can then solve for the total current by drawing a perpendicular line from the end of I_1 to I_{total} and breaking the triangle into two
right triangles, as shown in Figure 6.6.

Since I_1 and I_2 are equal in magnitude and the angle between them is
120°, we know that the angle θ is 60° because the perpendicular line
bisects the angle between I_1 and I_2. We also know that the side opposite
θ is half of I_{total} for the same reason. Therefore, we can use the formula
for the sine of an angle.

$$\sin\theta = \text{Opposite side} \div \text{Hypotenuse}$$

$$\sin 60° = (I_{total}/2) \div I_1$$

$$I_1 \times 0.866 = I_{total}/2$$

$$I_{total} = 2 \times I_1 \times 0.866$$

$$I_{total} = 1.732 \times I_1$$

Notice that if we had simply added I_1 and I_2 we would get $2 \times I_1$ or
$2 \times I_2$, provided it's a balanced three-phase system and $I_1 = I_2$. But since

I_1 and I_2 are 120° out of phase with each other, the total current in a conductor carrying both of these currents is only $1.732 \times I_1$.

The purpose of this exercise is to illustrate how two sinewaves that are out of phase with each other, in this case the two currents, do not add in a straightforward manner. On the opposite end of the spectrum, if they are completely out of phase with each other, then they will cancel. But if they are somewhat out of phase with each other, then the sum of the magnitude will be somewhere between 0 and twice the magnitude of one of them (assuming they are equal in magnitude).

In a three-phase system, there are two commonly used ways of wiring the three phases, as we will see later on. Both wiring methods use a common node between phases. Therefore, each of the three conductors carries the vectorial sum of two currents. As a result, the final formula for calculating the power in a balanced three-phase system is:

$$\text{Three-phase balanced AC power (watts)} = \text{Voltage (volts)} \times \text{Current (amps)} \times \text{Power factor} \times 1.73,$$

where the power factor is the cosine of the phase angle.

93

UNDERSTANDING AC POWER

6.1 If the phase angle between the voltage and the current is 30°, what is value of the real power as a percentage of maximum?

6.2 Why is the amount of power that is used zero when the voltage and current are 90° out of phase with each other?

6.3 What does a negative value of power imply?

6.4 When is the value of AC power and the value of DC power the same?

6.5 What is the phase angle when the power factor is 0.9125? (Hint: To find the angle for which the cosine is 0.9125, use the inverse function on your calculator.)

6.6 What is the power factor if the phase angle between the voltage and current is 50°?

6.7 Is it possible to have a power factor greater than 1? Why or why not?

6.8 Why is a low power factor undesirable?

6.9 Why is a luminaire with a high power factor smaller and lighter than an equivalent one with a lower power factor?

6.10 How can a low power factor be corrected?

6.11 If, in a highly reactive load, the current is high but the consumed power is low, what happens to the power in the system?

6.12 What is wattless power?

6.13 What is real power?

6.14 What is complex power?

6.15 If a load draws 13 amps at 120 volts, what is the apparent power?

6.16 If an HMI power supply has a power factor of 0.93 and draws 8.3 amps at 220 volts, then what is the phase angle? What is the real power? What is the reactive power?

6.17 If a transformer has a nameplate rating of 15 kVA and 2.5 kVAR, what is the real power? Phase angle?

6.18 If a 208V three-phase hoist draws 5 amps and has a power factor of 0.9, what is the three-phase power consumption?

6.19 A 41.7-horsepower three-phase motor has an efficiency of 94%. If there are 746 horsepower per watt, how many watts does the motor use?

6.20 If the three-phase motor above has a power factor of 0.80, how much current does it draw?

CHAPTER 7

Electrical Safety

Until this chapter of this book, we have discussed the theory of electricity and explored the relationship between voltage, current, resistance, and power. Now we will begin to explore the more practical application of electricity in the world of performing arts production. But before we do, we will take a detour through a short course in electrical safety and the effects of electricity on the human body. It's important to recognize the dangers involved with electricity and to maintain a healthy respect for it.

ELECTRIC SHOCK

There are many factors that influence the severity of the electrical shock that results when a person comes into contact with a live conductor. These factors include voltage, current, waveform, whether it's alternating current or direct current, the frequency of AC, and the length of time of exposure. In addition, the impedance of the human body has a direct effect on the severity of the shock. The average person has an impedance of about 1000 ohms from one hand to the other, but this can vary depending on body shape, age, weight, sex, the path of the current through the body (if it's other than hand to hand), the amount of clothing worn, and the amount of moisture involved.

It doesn't take much current to make a human heart go into defibrillation. The body's own natural electrical pulses that pace the heart are on the order of a millionth of an amp. As little as 100 to 300 milliamps passing though the heart can interrupt its natural rhythm and cause it to go into fibrillation. When that happens, the heart flutters and can't deliver the necessary oxygen to the blood, eventually causing death.

Fortunately, we have a certain amount of control over the impedance we present to a power source. We can increase our impedance by wearing protective clothing, including V-rated gloves, rubber-soled shoes, long pants and shirt made of cotton (rather than nylon or other synthetic fabrics that will melt to the skin), a hat — preferably a hard hat or some other insulating material — and thick socks. We can take off dangling jewelry like necklaces or earrings, and carry a carpet to stand on in the event our work environment is bare concrete. We can use V-rated tools and we can ensure that we are not standing in water when we're working on live electrical equipment.

In addition to trying to increase our impedance as much as possible, it also helps to be aware of the effects of the path that current takes through the human body. The most damage is caused by electricity passing through the lungs, heart, and brain. But the path of the highest impedance is from one hand to the other. Based on a factor of 1.0 for this path, Table 7.1 shows the relative reduction in impedance for alternate paths.

By taking precautions and working intelligently, we can lower our risk of electrocution. According to Ohm's law, if we can raise our impedance, then we will lower the current passing through our body in the unfortunate event that we come into contact with a live circuit. If we succeed in lowering the current then we have a better chance of survival.

EFFECTS OF ELECTRICAL CURRENT

Electrical current is what can cause damage to the human body. Its effects range from slight perception to heavy burns. Most people start to per-

Table 7.1	Relative Body Impedance Multipliers
Path	**Impedance factor**
Hand to hand	1.0
Hand to foot	1.0
Hand to head	0.5
Hand to chest	0.45
Hand to stomach	0.5
Hand to knee	0.7

ceive current at about 0.2 to 0.5 milliamps. The "startle" current is considered 0.5 milliamps. Although this level of current will most likely not cause any serious damage, if you're walking a truss or hanging off of a ladder it could be a very serious situation. At a level of 10 milliamps, 1.5% of men, 40% of women, and 92.5% of children contract their muscles to the point where they can't let go. At 20 mA, 92.5% of men and 100% of women and children can't let go. At 30 mA, no one can let go. The maximum current level allowable for every person to be able to let go is 6 mA, which is the trip value of a certain class of ground fault circuit interrupters (GFCIs) that are designed to protect human life. A current of 10 mA to 60 mA passing through the human body can cause difficulty in breathing. Should someone become frozen to a live conductor, they could stop breathing long enough to suffocate.

ARC FLASH AND ARC BLAST

In addition to the hazards of direct electrical shock, the production electrician faces other hazards as well, including arc flash and arc blast. In fact, according the National Fire Protection Association (NFPA), most electrical accidents that require admission to the hospital are caused by arc flash burns, not because of electrical shock. In the United States alone, over 2000 people are admitted to burn centers with severe burns due to arc flash each year.

An arc flash is when the air around a conductor becomes ionized and changes from an insulator to a conductor. When that happens, the live

conductor can discharge through the air to another live conductor or to a grounded conductor. The surrounding air can erupt in a plasma ball that engulfs the air and then dissipates in a fraction of a second. The temperature of the air can reach 19,427°C (35,000°F). If anyone is unfortunate enough to be in the arc flash zone, they could be severely burned.

In addition to the danger of the flash, an arcing conductor can produce an explosive blast with tremendous pressure. In the presence of the ultra-high temperatures produced by an arc flash, copper can vaporize and expand 67,000 times, producing a shower of molten metal. The blast can reach thousands of pounds per square foot and cause great damage,

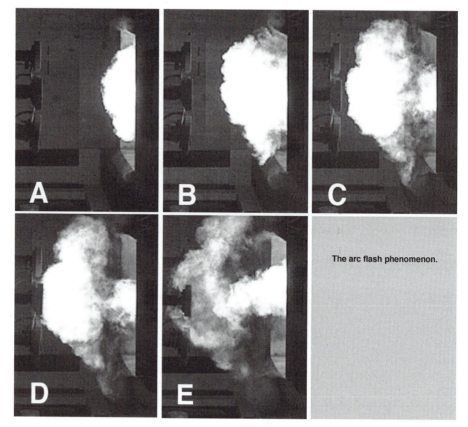

The arc flash phenomenon.

FIGURE 7.1
Arc flash sequence shown at 1-millisecond intervals. This is a 480-volt system. (Photo courtesy of Ferraz Shawmut.)

including ruptured eardrums, collapsed lungs, concussions, and internal organ ruptures.

The likelihood of an arc flash increases as the voltage increases: the higher the voltage the more likely it could happen. The size of the flash also depends on the voltage — the higher the voltage, the larger the arc flash — as well as the impedance of the circuit feeding it and the available fault current.

FIGURE 7.2
Arc flash picture taken at 10,000 frames per second. (Courtesy of Ferraz Shawmut High-Power Labs.)

An arc can be initiated by several triggers. Dust, impurities, and corrosion of insulators can initiate an arc and cause it to flash over. Water condensation or dripping water can also create a conductive path for an arc to flash over. Sometimes arcs are caused by a person accidentally touching a live part or dropping a tool into live equipment. Conductors can also flash over if the voltage is high enough and the gap to another conductor or ground is short enough. And sometimes the insulating material breaks down, allowing an arc to jump through it or around it.

NFPA 70E – Standard for Electrical Safety in the Workplace spells out the flash protection boundary within which a person could receive a second degree burn in the event of an arc flash. For under 300 volts, the flash protection boundary is 4 feet, although unqualified personnel are not allowed within 10 feet unless they are escorted by a qualified person.

We can't predict when an accident like an arc flash will take place, but there are steps we can take to protect ourselves in the event of such an accident. When we're working around live electrical equipment we can wear protective clothing such as flame-resistant (FR) clothing and V-rated gloves (gloves rated and tested for a particular voltage), and use V-rated tools. We can also wear clothing made with non-melting fabrics, such as cotton, and avoid wearing clothing made with fabric that will melt with excessive heat, such as nylon, polyester, spandex, and other synthetic fabrics.

LOCKOUT/TAGOUT

The lockout/tagout procedure, as described in NFPA 70E Article 120, Establishing an Electrically Safe Work Condition, is a way of ensuring an electrically safe working environment when work needs to be done on an electrical system. The aim of the procedure is to achieve safe working conditions by interrupting the load current and disconnecting the circuit from the source, verifying that circuits are properly de-energized, locking out or tagging out according to the established policy, and testing each part of the circuit with a voltage detector from phase to phase and phase to ground before anyone begins working on an electrical system. In the case where there might be stored energy, for example, in large capacitor banks or where there is the possibility that voltage can be induced, the phase conductors should be grounded by connecting them to ground with devices rated to handle the fault current. NFPA 70E also requires that employers have a written plan for lockout/tagout procedures and that they train employees in the procedures.

There are three classifications of hazardous electrical energy control procedures: individual qualified employee control, simple lockout/tagout, and complex lockout/tagout. When equipment is de-energized for minor maintenance, servicing, adjusting, cleaning, inspection, and such work, then a qualified individual can do the work without placing a lock or tag on the disconnect provided the disconnect is adjacent to the work, the employee can clearly see the disconnect while performing the work, and the work doesn't extend beyond one shift.

Any work that doesn't fall under individual qualified employee control procedures or complex lockout/tagout procedures is considered a simple lockout/tagout procedure. It requires that up-to-date single-line drawings of the electrical system are used to identify all sources of energy. Then the load is de-energized and a lock is placed on the equipment to prevent it from being re-energized until it is ready to be returned to service. In cases where the equipment doesn't allow the use of a lock, the tagout procedure is used with at least one other safety precaution. Any stored energy should be released, including spring-loaded mechanisms such as large circuit breakers, and it should be verified that equipment cannot be restarted by operating any motor switches or the like. The voltage should then be measured to confirm the circuit is not live and grounding devices should be installed for the duration of the work should they be required.

If there are multiple sources of energy, multiple crews, multiple crafts, multiple locations, multiple employers, different means of disconnection, or a particular sequence requirement, or if the work will continue beyond one work shift, then it is considered a complex lockout/tagout procedure. It requires that a qualified person is appointed with overall responsibility and that a plan of execution is written out.

FIGURE 7.3
Lockout/tagout procedure ensures that equipment is de-energized, locked out, and tested before anyone works on it.

Most disconnects will accommodate a padlock in order to lock the switch in the "off" position, and equipment that was installed after January 2, 1990 is required to accept a lockout device. The lock can be a keyed lock or a combination lock, and the key or combination should stay with the person who installed the lock or, in the event of an established procedure, with the person in charge. The lock has to have a label or some other means of identifying the individual who installed it, and it should be accompanied by a tag stating that unauthorized personnel are prohibited from removing the device or operating the disconnect. It should also be suitable for the environment and for the duration of the work to be performed.

There are many other requirements and procedures involved in a safe lockout/tagout program, and this text is not intended to replace the NFPA 70E Article 120. There is also a sample lockout/tagout procedure in Annex G that describes in detail each step to be taken during a lockout. If you are involved in the installation, maintenance, or repair of electrical equipment, then it is a good idea to obtain a copy of NFPA 70E by visiting www.nfpa.org.

Such formal procedures may seem unnecessary or even ridiculous at times, but when it comes to safety, we can't afford to make mistakes. Even though the vast majority of us work with voltage levels under 600 volts, it is still potentially dangerous work. Of the approximately

1000 fatalities that occur in the United States each year due to electrocution, more than half are caused by less than 600 volts. Never let down your guard. Always be vigilant around electricity.

DRUGS AND ALCOHOL

Working safely around electrical and electronic gear is a matter of knowledge and good judgment. It requires a sharp mind and quick reflexes. The production environment is a dangerous place in which to bring drugs and alcohol, not only for the user, but also for everyone involved in the show, including the audience. For the sake of the safety of everyone involved, keep all drugs and alcohol away from the work environment. Even some prescription and over-the-counter drugs that cause drowsiness should be avoided while you're on the job. Every production and event is a potential safety hazard and deserves to be treated with care and the utmost attentiveness.

UNDERSTANDING ELECTRICAL SAFETY

7.1   Name at least three factors that influence the impedance of the human body.

7.2   What is the approximate impedance of the average person?

7.3   What is fibrillation?

7.4   How much current does it take to make the heart go into fibrillation?

7.5   Name at least three ways to increase your impedance as presented to a power source.

7.6   Why should you wear cotton clothing rather than synthetic fiber clothing when you are working around electricity?

7.7   Which of your vital organs is most susceptible to damage due to electric shock?

7.8   If the impedance from one hand to the other is 1000 ohms, what would be the impedance from the hand to the head?

7.9   What is the perception current?

7.10   How much current does it take to startle the average person?

7.11   If the startle current does not injure a person, why is it dangerous?

7.12   At what level of current is any person unable to let go?

7.13   Why do some electricians use the back of their hand to make sure a circuit is dead?

7.14   At what level of current does a person have difficulty breathing?

7.15   What is the most common injury due to an electrical accident?

7.16   What is an arc flash?

7.17   What is the temperature of the air in the event of an arc flash?

7.18   What is an arc blast?

7.19   What happens to copper when it is exposed to the kinds of temperatures produced by an arc flash?

7.20   Name at least three injuries commonly caused by an arc blast.

7.21   Name at least three things that can contribute to arc flash.

7.22   What is the definition of the flash protection boundary?

7.23   What is the arc flash boundary for under 300 volts?

7.24   What is lockout/tagout?

7.25   Why is it important that only one person keeps the key in a lockout/tagout?

"Technology: no place for wimps!"

Dilbert

It is often said that electricity always returns to its source. How it returns is a matter of considerable importance when it comes to safety. An improperly grounded/earthed system offers ample opportunity for personnel to get between the source and its return path. But a properly grounded/earthed system is designed to provide maximum protection for personnel and equipment.

In the 1970s, when amplified musical instruments and public address systems were relatively new, few people understood how to build safe power distribution systems. As a result, there were at least three high-profile musicians who were electrocuted by their equipment because of improper grounding/earthing (Leslie Harvey of Stone the Crows, John Rostill of the Shadows, and Keith Relf of the Yardbirds). Today, we know much more about proper grounding/earthing techniques and electrical safety. Understanding grounding/earthing techniques is a very important and somewhat complex issue. Volumes have been written on the subject and it is still being debated and evolving. Nevertheless, there are certain principles that are well understood.

THE COMPLETE CIRCUIT

In order for current to flow, two conditions must be satisfied: (1) there must be a voltage or potential difference between two points in the circuit, and (2) there must be a complete path for the current to flow between the two points. If there is a complete, uninterrupted path, it is referred to as a complete circuit or a closed circuit. If the circuit is interrupted and the current doesn't have a complete path, it is referred to as an open circuit.

FIGURE 8.1
Symbols for ground or earth.

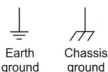

Signal ground   Earth ground   Chassis ground

EARTHING/GROUNDING

The production electrician most commonly builds a complete circuit by interconnecting various cables and components of a power distribution system. When the system is fully assembled, there will be at least two cables that complete the path from one terminal of the power source to another. Somewhere in the circuit, usually where the power enters the building or at the utility pole, there will also be at least one point where one of the conductors, called the neutral, is connected to ground or earth through a stake, called a grounding electrode, that is driven into the earth. In addition to the neutral conductor, there is also an equipment grounding conductor (or a circuit protective conductor, as it is called in Europe) that serves to protect personnel and equipment by keeping it at zero potential. The symbols for ground/earth are shown in Figure 8.1.

ZERO-VOLT REFERENCE

Voltage is only meaningful when it is referenced to another point. When a bird lands on a high-voltage wire, it doesn't get electrocuted because it does not complete a circuit to a zero-voltage reference or to another point in the circuit with a different potential. If the bird happens to straddle the gap between the high-voltage line and the metal transmission tower or another line, sparks will fly. That's because the voltage needs a reference.

We typically take zero volts as the absolute reference for voltage measurement. The exception is when we want to know the voltage drop across a particular component such as a resistor or a transistor. But normally, for example, a 12-volt DC power supply means that the positive terminal is 12 volts higher than a zero-volt reference. When we say a voltage rail is at 5 volts, that implies that is has been referenced against zero volts and it is 5 volts below the reference. Without some reference point with which to compare, voltage measurements are meaningless.

But what is our zero-volt reference based on?

The zero-volt reference is the earth, the largest current sink available to us. The earth is actually a conductor, although various parts of it are better conductors than others. Soil composition, moisture content, mineral content, and other factors influence the impedance of the soil at any given location. But the earth is a very large current sink, and as long as we can establish good contact with it, we have a good zero-volt reference. Every power distribution system has at least one point that is electrically connected to the earth, usually by means of a copper rod driven into the ground. We call this zero-volt reference ground in North America, earth in Europe and Australia.

FIGURE 8.2
The earth is the zero-volt reference for power distribution systems. In North America and other countries it's called ground, and in Europe, Australia, and other countries it is called earth.

VOLTAGE STABILITY

In an AC power distribution system, grounding or earthing is the practice of connecting one side of the power source to a low resistance path to the ground (or to the earth) in order to create a stable zero-volt reference. A grounding or earthing rod is mechanically and electrically connected, or bonded, to the power system, usually at the point of entry into the building (also known as the service entrance). Not only does the rod provide a stable zero-volt reference, but it also helps to limit the voltage on the system. In the event of a lightning strike, power surge, or a short circuit, the earth acts as a sink and the surge is absorbed.

SAFETY GROUNDING

A properly grounded or earthed power distribution system includes an equipment grounding conductor, also known as a circuit protective conductor (CPC) in Europe, which is bonded with an unspliced main bonding jumper to the grounded conductor inside of the service disconnect enclosure. The equipment grounding conductor, or CPC, is usually the green or green/yellow striped conductor, or a bare copper wire in the United States and Canada. It serves to provide a low-impedance path to ground in the event of a ground fault and to keep everything connected to it at ground potential. A ground fault is any unintentional contact between a live conductor and a grounded object. If the system is properly grounded, then the grounding conductor will cause a large current to flow to the earth, thereby tripping the overcurrent protection device or fuse and de-energizing the circuit. The main bonding jumper serves to carry the ground fault current from the service enclosure and the grounding conductor back to its source.

If the circuit is not properly grounded, then a ground fault will cause the metal chassis or housing to be energized but no current will flow; the overcurrent device will be of no help. If someone comes along and touches the chassis or housing while simultaneously touching a grounded object, for example, a microphone or guitar strings, then that person will complete the circuit to ground and current will flow through the person. It's a potentially lethal situation. For that reason, it is not a good idea to lift a ground on any piece of gear.

Equipment enclosures and current-carrying conductive parts are bonded together and to the system grounding conductor in order to keep everything at ground or earth potential. This also protects equipment by preventing high-impedance faults from causing damage. Without a low-impedance path to the earth, a high-impedance fault, such as arcing from a live wire to a metal pipe, could cause a low current to flow, producing too little current to trip the overcurrent protection but enough current to burn through a conductor or start a fire.

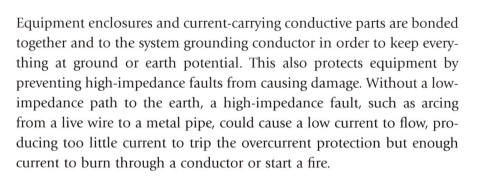

FIGURE 8.3
Proper grounding techniques help prevent accidental injury by causing a large current to flow to ground in the event of a ground fault, thus tripping the circuit breaker. In this illustration, a ground fault on an improperly grounded chassis creates a dangerous situation. The man touching the energized chassis completes the path to ground and becomes part of the circuit.

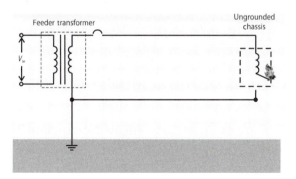

FIGURE 8.4
An improperly grounded chassis presents a low-impedance path to ground, causing a low current to flow in some instances. If the current is not high enough to trip the circuit breaker, it could persist and eventually burn through a wire or cause a fire.

All of the metallic components of a power distribution system and the metal enclosures of connected loads should be bonded to the system grounding conductor to ensure that there is a low-impedance path to the earth.

GROUNDED VERSUS GROUNDING VERSUS BONDING

In electrical parlance, certain terms relating to grounding are commonly confused. The neutral (the white or gray wire in North America, the blue wire in Europe, the black wire in India and Australia, and the light blue wire in China) is grounded at the panelboard, so it is referred to as a grounded conductor. None of the phase conductors are grounded, so they are referred to as ungrounded conductors. The grounding conductor is usually the green or green/yellow striped wire, or it can be a bare copper wire in the United States and Canada. Grounding is a continual process — the system is constantly kept at zero potential — so the green wire is called the grounding wire as opposed to the neutral, which is the grounded conductor.

Bonding is the physical connection between metallic conducting materials in the system such as metal enclosures, conduit, and water pipes. The components of a power distribution system are bonded to ensure that they remain at ground potential and to provide a low-impedance path to ground. The grounded wire (neutral) is connected to the grounding wire (green or green/yellow striped wire) using a main bonding jumper in the service-disconnect enclosure.

Of course, the term ground is an American term meaning earth. In other countries, the term earth is used in favor of ground.

UNI-GROUNDING VERSUS MULTI-GROUNDING

A power distribution system that is grounded or earthed at only one point is called a uni-grounded system in North America and a TN-S (terra-neutral-single earth) system in Europe. If the system is grounded or earthed in more than one place, then the return path for any ground fault current is through the earth. The size of the fault current, therefore, depends on the impedance of the earth between the two grounding electrodes. The value of impedance can vary depending on the soil con-

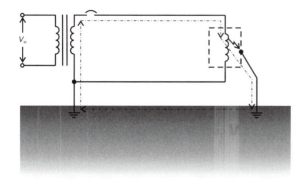

FIGURE 8.5
Earthing or grounding at two points means that the return path for a ground fault current is through the earth, as shown by the dotted and dashed line. Depending on the soil condition, the impedance of the earth may not allow enough current to flow to trip the overcurrent protection device.

ditions and the distance between the grounding electrodes. If the impedance is too high, then a ground fault will not produce enough current to trip the overcurrent protective device (or breaker) and there will be a potentially deadly situation.

To address this issue, residual current devices (RCDs) are often used to help mitigate accidents. A RCD is a circuit interruption device that can sense the difference between the outgoing current and the return current. If it detects such a leakage current of 30 milliamps or more, it will interrupt the circuit. Thus, if there is a ground fault where the ground fault current is not high enough to trip the overcurrent protection device, the RCD will stop it.

GROUND LOOPS

Audio hum and noise are the bane of the audio professional's existence. Those pesky noise problems are related to the system ground in that they are often caused by current flowing in a loop through the grounding wire and signal shield. Ground loops can degrade lighting control signals as well. Following good grounding practices and understanding how ground loops occur will keep the system safe and help minimize or eliminate problems with ground loops.

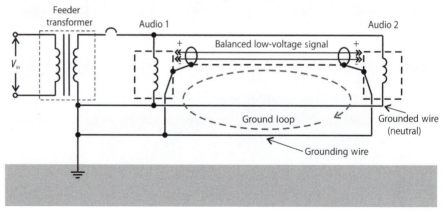

FIGURE 8.6

A ground loop enabled by a connection between the system grounding conductor, the chassis ground, and signal ground. Grounding loops can cause hum in audio systems and degrade control signals.

There are normally three distinct grounding entities in an audio system: the power distribution system ground, the equipment chassis ground, and the signal ground. If these three entities are all interconnected, they can form a loop through which current can flow.

The easiest—and the most dangerous—way to interrupt a ground loop is to lift the ground using a three-to-two prong adaptor. This method breaks the current path, but it puts personnel at great risk of electrocution. A ground fault can energize the equipment, and any unfortunate person who happens to make contact with the equipment and ground (or a grounded conductor) can be seriously injured or killed. A much better way to handle the situation is to leave the grounding wires intact and use another method to interrupt the ground loop. Alternatives include using a telescoping shield (connect the signal shield on only one end of the cable), isolation transformers, or balanced power (see the following section, page 113) with a center-tapped secondary, which causes ground loops to cancel.

BALANCED POWER SYSTEMS

In the Unites States, NEC code allows for the use of balanced power in a separately derived system (meaning that it has its own service, whether from a different feeder transformer, generator, or another system) that

provides two balanced phases of opposite polarity. Because the lines are inverted in phase, the line to ground voltage is 60 volts and the line-to-line voltage is 120 volts. The purpose of this system is to ensure that any noise that is picked up equally on the two phases is cancelled. It does so because the noise is summed in the ground, and if it is equal in magnitude but opposite in phase, the result is zero.

FIGURE 8.7
A balanced output transformer causes ground loops to cancel because they circulate through both halves of the secondary in equal magnitude but in opposite polarity.

These systems are only allowed in commercial or industrial buildings where their use can be restricted to qualified personnel. They can use standard panelboards as long as the voltage rating exceeds the voltage of the system and is clearly marked on the outside of the panel or inside the doors of the panel. Two-pole breakers must be used because each branch circuit has two live wires.

Receptacles and permanently installed equipment in this system have to have an equipment ground that is connected to an equipment grounding bus in the panelboard, and it must be marked "Technical Equipment Ground." It has to be connected to the grounded conductor (neutral) but it doesn't have to be bonded to the panelboard enclosure. Also, receptacles have to be protected by GFCIs (see the section titled "Ground Fault Circuit Interrupters" in Chapter 9, page 126) and must be marked as follows:

WARNING – TECHNICAL POWER
Do not connect to lighting equipment.
For electronic equipment use only.

60/120 V. 1ϕac
GFCI protected

There must also be a standard 125-volt, single-phase, 15- or 20-amp outlet within 6 feet of every 60/120V technical power outlet. Isolated ground receptacles can be used provided they are installed according to applicable codes.

There are more requirements for meeting code for balanced power systems, but the details are beyond the scope of this book. Refer to *NEC Article 647 – Sensitive Electronic Equipment* for more information.

113

TECHNICAL EARTH/TECHNICAL GROUND

In a low-voltage DC system primarily concerned with signal processing, whether it's an audio, video, or lighting control signal, the ground or earth is distinguished from a power distribution ground/earth by the term technical ground or technical earth. A technical ground/ earth is a grounding system that is isolated from the power distribution grounding system. It is reserved for a single purpose such as audio or video processing in order to provide a "clean" supply of power free of electrical noise or interference that could compromise the integrity of a signal.

UNDERSTANDING GROUNDING CONCEPTS

8.1 What two conditions must be satisfied before current can flow?

8.2 A _____ _____ is a circuit in which there is a closed path for the flow of current.

8.3 What is the purpose of grounding or earthing the neutral conductor?

8.4 What is the purpose of the equipment grounding conductor?

8.5 Voltage needs a _____ _____ in order to be meaningful.

8.6 What would happen if a live conductor were to make contact with a metal equipment enclosure that is not properly grounded?

8.7 How are equipment enclosures and non-current-carrying conductive parts kept at zero potential?

8.8 Another word for "ground" is _____.

8.9 What is another term for the grounded conductor?

8.10 What is the difference between the grounded conductor and the grounding conductor?

8.11 What is the difference between bonding and grounding?

8.12 The point at which the power distribution system enters a building is called the _____ _____.

8.13 What is the difference between a uni-grounded system and a multi-grounded system?

8.14 What is the potential hazard associated with a multi-grounded system? How is it usually addressed?

8.15 Why does lifting the ground on a piece of gear put personnel at risk of electrocution?

CHAPTER 9
Overcurrent and Undercurrent Protection

To borrow from Dominique Bouhours, electricity is a good servant but a cruel master. For that reason, it pays to take extra care in building power distribution systems and using electricity. Over the years, measures have been developed and refined for the proper use and construction of these systems. One of the most important aspects of the safe distribution of electricity is the proper use of overcurrent protection. There are two primary types of overcurrent protection: fuses and circuit breakers.

FUSES

A fuse is a calibrated weak link in a circuit that will predictably and reliably melt when a predetermined magnitude of current is reached for a designated duration. When the fuse element melts, the circuit is interrupted and the current will cease to flow. There is an inverse-time relationship between the size of the current and the time it takes to blow: the higher the current, the faster the fuse will open.

Fuses are sized according to their rated current and voltage. The current rating of a fuse should be between 0 and 30% higher than the continuous operating current in the circuit, depending on the type of fuse and the standard to which it complies. Fuses used in North America typically comply with Underwriters Laboratories (UL) and/or Canadian Standards Association (CSA) standard 248-14 for low-voltage fuses (under 600V), while those used in Europe comply with International Electrotechnical Commission (IEC) standard 60127-2. UL and CSA standards are harmonized but they differ from IEC standards. Table 9.1 shows the allowable continuous operating current for various types of fuses at 23°C.

If the rated current of a fuse is undersized, then it is subject to nuisance tripping due to fluctuations and spikes in the line voltage. If it's oversized, it can be a potential fire hazard or a hazard to personnel by allowing too much current to flow. When you are replacing a fuse, it is important to use the same fuse type, since UL and CSA ratings are different from IEC ratings. For a 250V fuse, for example, a 1.4-amp UL/CSA fuse is approximately the same as a 1-amp IEC-rated fuse. Therefore, if a fuse manufactured to UL standards is replaced with a fuse manufactured to IEC standards, then the circuit will no longer be protected properly. And it goes without saying that it's never a good idea, regardless of the circumstances, to bypass a fuse with a chewing gum wrapper or any other conductive material.

Table 9.1	Allowable Continuous Operating Current for Fuses at 23°C	
Standard	**Voltage Rating**	**Allowable Continuous Operating Current (23°)**
UL/CSA	125V	Less than 70% of I_{rated}
UL/CSA	250V	Less than 75% of I_{rated}
IEC	125V	Less than 70% of I_{rated}
IEC	250V	Less than 100% of I_{rated}
IEC	32V–250V	Less than 80% of I_{rated}

(Courtesy of Wickmann, www.wickmann.com.)

It is also very important that the fuse is rated at or higher than the circuit voltage, or there is a risk of arcing across the open fuse terminals, thus bypassing the overcurrent protection. Furthermore, a fuse with the wrong voltage rating will work just fine until the fuse link blows and an arc is generated across the terminals. Therefore, it is extremely important to pay close attention to the current and voltage ratings of replacement fuses. A properly rated fuse is designed to withstand the open circuit voltage for 30 seconds after the fuse blows or to have an interrupt resistance of at least 1 k ohms.

There are several different types of fuses that are classified according to how quickly or how slowly they will open in a fault or overcurrent situation. A fast-acting normal fuse will blow more quickly than a time-delayed or time-lag fuse will; although, as you can see by Table 9.2, you can overload a fast-acting normal fuse by 50% and it might still take several minutes to blow. Time-delayed fuses are used in situations where the inrush current is high and the steady-state operating current is lower. Examples include discharge lamps, motors, transformers, and other highly capacitive or inductive loads.

In the power distribution systems that we typically deal with, we come across fuses on a regular basis in certain applications. The secondary sides of feeder transformers, for example, are sometimes fused. So are the inputs to some large permanently installed dimmer racks. They sometimes use large bolt-in fuses filled with quartz sand to quench the arc and absorb the heat generated by stopping large currents. This type of fuse is occasionally called by the trade name Amp-Trap.

Of course, many luminaires are fused with miniature fuses, and some connectors in the UK have built-in fuses. But the BS-546:1950 15 A connector is commonly used in theatres in the UK precisely because it doesn't have a fuse. And since every circuit is already protected by a fuse or circuit breaker in the dimmer, a second fuse in the connector is redundant and unnecessary. In fact, a second fuse in the same circuit makes it more difficult and time consuming to troubleshoot the circuit.

FIGURE 9.1
An Amp-Trap is a quartz sand-filled fuse for high current applications. (Photo courtesy of Ferraz Shawmut.)

Table 9.2   Miniature Fuse Time-Current Characteristics for UL/CSA and IEC Standards

% Rated Current	Current Range	UL/CSA 248-14		IEC 60127-2				
		Fast-Acting Normal Blow	Time-Delay	Quick-Acting I	Quick-Acting II	Time-Lag III	Time-Lag IV	Time-Lag V
100%	0–10 A	*	*					
135%	0–10 A	<1 hour	<1 hour					
150%	50 mA–6.3 A, 32 mA–6.3 A, 1 A–6.3 A			<1 hour	<1 hour	<1 hour	<1 hour	<1 hour
200%	0–10 A, 0–3 A	<2 min	<5 s					
210%	50 mA–6.3 A, 32 mA–6.3 A, 1 A–6.3 A			<30 min	<30 min	<2 min	<30 min	<2 min
275%	50 mA–3.15 A, 4 A–6.3 A, 32 mA–100 mA, 125 mA–6.3 A, 1 A–6.3 A			10 ms–2 s, 10 ms–3 s	10 ms–500 ms, 50 ms–2 s	200 ms–10 s, 600 ms–10 s	1 s–80 s	200 ms–10 s, 600 ms–10 s
400%	50 mA–3.15 A, 32 mA–100 mA, 125 mA–6.3 A, 1 A–3.15 A, 4 A–6.3 A			3 ms–300 ms	3 ms–100 ms, 10 ms–300 ms	40 ms–3 s, 150 ms–3 s	95 ms–5 s, 150 ms–5 s	40 ms–3 s, 150 ms–3 s
1000%	50 mA–6.3 A, 32 mA–6.3 A, 32 mA–100 mA, 125 mA–6.3 A, 1 A–3.15 A, 4 A–6.3 A			<20 ms	<20 ms	10 ms–300 ms, 20 ms–300 ms	10 ms–100 ms, 20 ms–100 ms	10 ms–300 ms, 20 ms–300 ms

Every part of a power distribution system should have some form of overcurrent protection. If it doesn't have a fuse, then it should have a circuit breaker.

The very first standard for "Electric Light Wires, Lamps, etc." in the United States was written by the New York Board of Fire Underwriters in 1881. It had five simple rules for installers: (1) use wires with 50% more ampacity than the connected load, (2) use wires that are "insulated and doubly coated with some approved material," (3) fasten the wires with approved non-conducting fasteners every 2-1/2" for incandescent lamps and every 8" for arc lamps, 8" from all other wires or metal conductive surfaces in the open where they can be inspected, (4) protect arc lamps with glass globes to prevent sparks or hot carbon from causing a fire, and (5) use a shut-off switch at the point of entrance of the electricity into a building and turn off the power when not in use. It went on to say that an application to use electric lights must be accompanied by a statement of the number of lamps to be used, an estimate from "some known electrician" of the "quantity of electricity required," a sample of at least 3 feet of the wire to be used, a certificate of the ampacity of the wire, and information about where the electricity would be generated, whether or not the circuit would have a ground, and the details of the installation.

Edison understood the dangers of bringing electricity into homes and businesses. Though he wrote a letter to the New York Board of Fire Underwriters exclaiming that his DC power generation, distribution, and lighting system were "absolutely free from any possible danger from fire," he recognized that if the current exceeded the ampacity of the wire then it would indeed be dangerous. Therefore, he designed his system to minimize that danger by inventing the fusible link or fuse. As early as 1883, Edison's systems used a "breakdown plug," or what we now call a fuse.

CIRCUIT BREAKERS

A circuit breaker is a resettable switch that opens and closes a circuit manually or automatically in the event of an overload or short circuit. They are necessitated by the governing body in virtually every location in the civilized world — the National Electrical Code (NEC) in the United States, the Canadian Standards Association (CSA) in Canada, the "Wiring Regs" or BS7671: Requirements for Electrical Installations in the United Kingdom, and the International Electrotechnical Commission (IEC) in the European Union, to name but a few.

In the live event production industry, we normally deal with low-voltage (600 volts and under) circuit breakers, and usually the molded case variety, although miniature circuit breakers are occasionally found in automated luminaires and similar devices. Circuit breakers can be further classified according to the mode of operation. There are thermal, thermal-magnetic, magnetic, and electronic circuit breakers.

The typical circuit breaker most often found in North American power distribution systems is the thermal or thermal-magnetic type. The mechanism by which a thermal circuit breaker senses overload current is a bi-metallic strip through which the current flows. The strip is laminated with two dissimilar metals, each with a different coefficient of expansion. The current flowing through the metals causes them to heat up due to their resistance and they expand as they heat. Because each of the two metal strips has a different coefficient of expansion, they expand at different rates, causing the laminated strip to bend. When the current reaches a predetermined magnitude the bi-metallic strip will bend enough to trigger a spring-loaded switch, which then opens the contacts and breaks the circuit.

Thermal circuit breakers are affected by the ambient temperature because the amount of energy it takes to heat the bi-metallic strip to the tripping point depends on its starting temperature. Thermal breakers are somewhat forgiving of voltage spikes and surges because of the time it takes for the current to heat up the bi-metallic strip. A spike or surge of a few cycles will have no obvious effects on a thermal breaker. For that same reason, they are relatively slow to react to faults and short circuits. Therefore, some thermal circuit breakers have a magnetic relay to sense large currents and more quickly trigger the switch. These thermal-magnetic circuit breakers offer both overload protection (with a slower response) and short circuit protection (with a faster response time).

Magnetic circuit breakers are more common in Europe and are found to a lesser degree in North America. Rather than using a bi-metallic strip, magnetic circuit breakers sense current through a coil of wire or an inductor. The magnetic field generated by the current flowing through the inductor attracts a moveable iron core, which in turn can trigger a spring-loaded switch when the current is strong enough. This solenoid is very fast acting and very accurate.

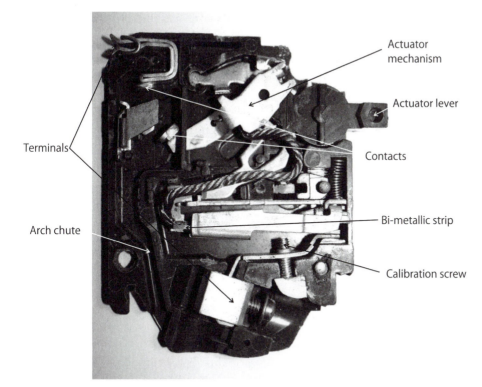

Actuator mechanism

Actuator lever

Terminals

Contacts

Arch chute

Bi-metallic strip

Calibration screw

FIGURE 9.2
A thermal circuit breaker has a bi-metallic strip that is calibrated to heat up and trip the switch in the event of an overload. The two metal strips have a different coefficient of expansion and expand at different rates due to the heat generated by the current flow.

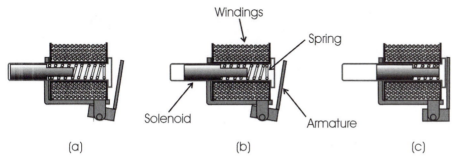

Windings

Spring

Solenoid

Armature

(a)   (b)   (c)

FIGURE 9.3
A magnetic circuit breaker senses current with a solenoid. The magnetic field of the inductor pushes a moveable core, which trips a spring-loaded switch at a predetermined current level. (a) A cross-sectional view of a magnetic circuit breaker with no load. (b) The same breaker with some load but under the trip threshold. (c) The same breaker beyond the threshold tripping current.

Some magnetic circuit breakers are filled with viscous fluid to introduce a slight delay to the reaction of the solenoid. This allows for brief periods of inrush currents and surges but provides for overload protection. Large short circuit currents are sufficient to overcome the hydraulic delay and trip the circuit breaker almost instantaneously.

Electronic circuit breakers replace the magnetic solenoid with a much faster and more accurate Hall sensor and digital processing. They are unaffected by the ambient air temperature and they can be designed to filter out harmonics, thus eliminating nuisance tripping due to harmonic currents.

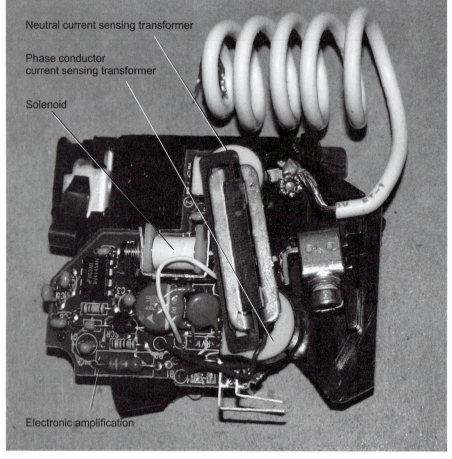

Neutral current sensing transformer

Phase conductor current sensing transformer

Solenoid

Electronic amplification

FIGURE 9.4
Magnetic GFCI breaker showing the two current sensors, solenoid, and electronics.

CIRCUIT BREAKER RATINGS

All circuit breakers have a voltage rating, a current rating, and a short circuit current rating. The voltage rating ensures that the device can safely interrupt a circuit at or below the rated voltage and extinguish the arc pulled by the interruption of current. Single-pole breakers are rated according to their maximum phase-to-ground voltage and multiple-pole breakers are rated according to their maximum phase-to-phase voltage.

Circuit breakers are inverse-time devices: the higher the overcurrent, the faster they trip. They are rated according to the maximum continuous (meaning 3 hours or more) current that the breaker can carry in free air. Since they end up mounted in an enclosure with limited air circulation, the actual maximum continuous current a thermal-magnetic breaker can carry is 80% of the rated current. This excludes circuit breakers that are integral to certain equipment such as dimmers and automated lighting. Electronic circuit breakers can generally operate at 100% of their rated current in continuous duty.

RESIDUAL CURRENT DEVICES

In North America, getting an occasional shock by the 120-volt household mains supply is almost a rite of passage. In Europe, where the mains supply is 230V or 240V, getting "bit" by the mains supply might lead to your last rites. The higher voltage is much more dangerous because it produces more current given the same impedance. In some parts of Europe, the situation is exacerbated by the fact that the utility companies use a T-T (terra-terra) earthing system whereby the electrical service is grounded at the service entrance or utility pole and at the point of consumption as well. The ground fault return path is taken to be the earth, and if it happened to be a less than ideal conductor, then so be it. The problem is that if the impedance of the return path for fault currents is high enough, then the current is proportionately lower. Since the circuit breakers that are supposed to protect the circuit from large short circuit currents have an inverse-time relationship with the current — the larger the current, the faster they act — they will not act as quickly as they would if the grounding conductor or circuit protective conductor were used to create a low-impedance path to the source. Thus, more damage can occur and personnel are at greater risk. Add to that the smaller, higher impedance wires used there because of the higher voltage and lower currents, and you have a recipe for mishap.

But the Germans, being the clever people they are, invented a solution to help curb the risk. Their earliest solution was to build high-precision "Swiss watch" 4X breakers. Whereas the typical circuit breaker required 7.5 to 20 times the rated current in order to trip instantaneously, the 4X breaker would trip instantaneously at four times its rated current. These breakers improved the situation but didn't completely resolve the problem.

Their second pass produced a new type of device that would detect ground faults of as little as 500 milliamps. Later, the sensitivity would improve to trip at 100 milliamps, and then improve again to trip at 30 milliamps. These devices use a donut-shaped current transformer through which all of the current-carrying conductors are run. If the vectorial sum of the outgoing current and the return current is equal to zero, then no control voltage is generated because the magnetic fields of the currents would cancel. However, in the event of a ground fault, not all of the outgoing current would be returned through the current transformer, thus signaling a problem. The voltage created by the current transformer would be used to trigger the circuit breaker to open. These so-called residual current devices, or RCDs, helped resolve the problems with ground faults in T-T systems.

GROUND FAULT CIRCUIT INTERRUPTERS

In 1962, Professor Charles Dalziel of the University of California at Berkeley learned about RCDs through his work in the area of electrical safety when he attended a meeting in Geneva, Switzerland. He subsequently teamed with a manufacturing company to help develop an improved version of an RCD with a lower trip level. By using an electronic control circuit instead of an electromechanical relay, they could more accurately monitor the differential current and they were able to build a device with a trip level of 15 milliamps. They called it a ground fault circuit interrupter (GFCI). By 1968, the National Electrical Code required the use of GFCIs in the circuits used for the underwater lighting of swimming pools.

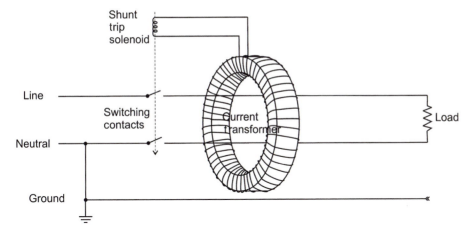

FIGURE 9.5

A residual current device has a current transformer through which the line and neutral wires are run. If the vectorial sum of the outgoing and return currents is zero, then no voltage is generated in the current transformer. In the event of a ground fault, the two currents don't add up to zero and the current transformer generates a voltage that causes the solenoid to open the switching contacts.

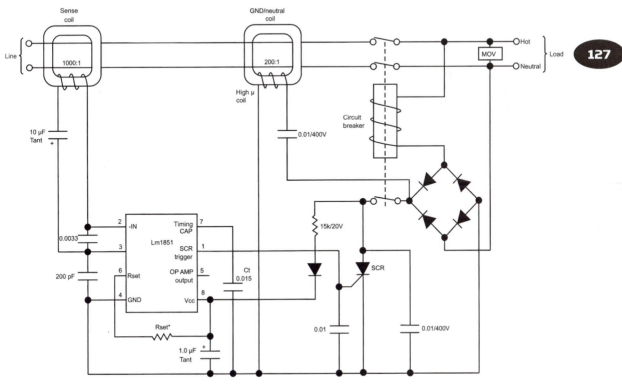

127

FIGURE 9.6

A GFCI is a type of RCD with electronic control. It has a "must trip" value of 6 milliamps and a "must not trip" value of 4 milliamps.

CLASS A GFCIS

Today, hundreds of millions of GFCIs are installed in electrical systems in North America. A harmonized tri-national standard defining Class A GFCIs was jointly issued by ANCE in Mexico as NMX J 520, CSA in Canada as CSA C22.2, and by UL in the United States as UL 943 in 2008. The standard describes Class A GFCIs as devices designed to protect 95% of normal healthy adults by interrupting a circuit when a ground fault current exceeds 6 milliamps. According to the standard, it must trip at 6 milliamps of leakage current and must not trip below 4 milliamps of leakage current. Since they are inverse-time devices, they react faster to higher currents. Class B GFCIs were the original GFCIs with a minimum trip current of 20 milliamps that were used in swimming pool lighting circuits. They have long since been obsolete, but there are still some installed and in use.

Since RCDs and earth leakage circuit breakers (ELCBs) have higher trip currents, they do not meet the standard of a Class A GFCI in North America. They are, however, considered personnel protection devices in some other countries.

Since the development of GFCIs, the live production event industry has been left to its own devices as to whether to use them or not. But now the Entertainment Services and Technology Association (ESTA) is working on *BSR E1.19, Recommended Practice for the Use of Class A Ground-Fault Circuit Interrupters (GFCIs) Intended for Personnel Protection in the Entertainment Industry.* This recommended practice spells out when, where, and how to use GFCIs in places of assembly, the production of film, video, and broadcast, theatrical productions, carnivals, fairs, and similar events in North America. It covers electrical services of 100 amps or less, 120–240 VAC single- and three-phase 60-Hz circuits where the voltage to ground does not exceed 150 VAC. Note that since the voltage to ground in Europe is 230 VAC or 240 VAC, this standard specifically excludes those systems.

In brief, the standard calls for the use of GFCIs in any outdoor, wet, or damp locations unless the circuit is for egress lighting, exit lighting, or emergency lighting systems, or if tripping the GFCI could cause injury.

Since the control circuit in a GFCI requires constant power, the use of standard GFCIs on dimmed circuits is not allowed. There are, however, special GFCIs with a separate non-dim input designed for use with certain dimmer racks.

FIGURE 9.7
ETC Sensor GFCI Dimmer Module. GFCIs require constant power for the control circuit. Standard GFCIs should not be used with dimmers. (Photo courtesy of ETC.)

There is another potential problem with using GFCIs in a dimming circuit. In a conventional forward phase-control dimmer, the waveform is altered by the switching action of the dimmer. The resulting waveform has a high third-order harmonic content (see the section titled "Third-Order Harmonics," Chapter 11, page 152) that the GFCI may interpret as a residual current and then switch off the circuit. In order to avoid this nuisance tripping, dimmer-rated GFCIs must sense peak current instead of RMS current.

UNDERSTANDING OVERCURRENT AND UNDERCURRENT PROTECTION

129

9.1 What is the relationship between the size of the current and the time it takes to blow a fuse?

9.2 Why do fuses have a voltage rating?

9.3 Can you replace an IEC fuse with a UL or CSA fuse? Why or why not?

9.4 According to UL/CSA fuse standards, if the continuous operating current is 16 amps, what size fuse should be used?

9.5 A properly rated fuse is designed to withstand the open circuit voltage for _____ seconds or to have an interrupt resistance of at least _____ ohms.

9.6 What is the purpose of using a time-delay fuse?

9.7 What is the purpose of filling a fuse with sand?

9.8 Describe the process by which a thermal breaker senses current and opens the circuit in the event of an overcurrent situation.

9.9 Why are thermal circuit breakers more forgiving of voltage spikes and surges?

9.10   What is the purpose of combining thermal overload protection with magnetic circuit protection?

9.11   Describe the process by which a magnetic circuit breaker operates.

9.12   Which type of circuit breaker is more accurate, thermal or magnetic?

9.13   How does the ambient temperature affect thermal circuit breakers? How does it affect magnetic circuit breakers?

9.14   What is a T-T power distribution system?

9.15   What is an RCD?

9.16   What is a GFCI?

9.17   What is the difference between an RCD and a GFCI?

9.18   What is the difference between a Class A and a Class B GFCI?

9.19   Does *BSR E1.19, Recommended Practice for the Use of Class A Ground-Fault Circuit Interrupters (GFCIs) Intended for Personnel Protection in the Entertainment Industry* cover European power distribution systems?

9.20   When and where should GFCIs be used?

9.21   Should GFCIs be used for branch circuits for lighting on an ice rink?

9.22   When should GFCIs not be used?

9.23   Why is the use of standard GFCIs disallowed for use in dimmed circuits?

9.24   Can a GFCI operate without an equipment grounding conductor?

9.25   What can a system grounding conductor protect against that a GFCI cannot?

CHAPTER 10
Power Distribution Systems

"The new electronic interdependence recreates the world in the image of a global village."
Marshall McLuhan, from his book, *Gutenberg Galaxy*, 1962

Modern power distribution systems were developed long before Marshall McLuhan's observation of the world as a "global village." Power distribution systems are, in fact, the infrastructure upon which the Information Age was built. But they were developed in a time when people and countries were more isolated and standardization was in its infancy. As a result, there was a vast array of power distribution schemes and implementations before some standardization and harmonization reduced that number to a handful.

In North America, a variety of service connections can be encountered, depending on how old the construction is and whether it was constructed as a residential building, as a commercial building, as a performing arts center, or for some other use. Newer performing arts centers, theatres, and performance spaces almost always have a three-phase four-wire service connected in a wye or star configuration with a grounded neutral.

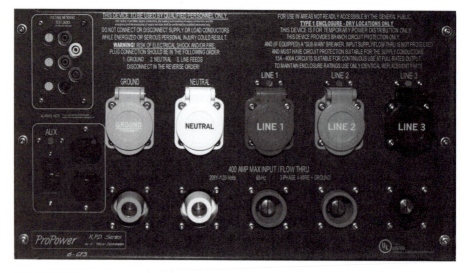

FIGURE 10.1
Typical portable power distribution rack showing color-coded power connections for a three-phase four-wire plus ground system. (Courtesy of AC Power Distribution, Inc., www.acpowerdistribution.com.)

THREE-PHASE FOUR-WIRE PLUS GROUND WYE OR STAR

A three-phase four-wire plus ground "wye" configuration, also known as a "star," is the most common secondary connection used in modern buildings and performance venues in North America, the European Union, Australia, South Africa, and many other parts of the world. It has three phase conductors, a neutral, which is normally grounded at the service entrance, and a ground, and they all have a common connection point or node, as shown in Figure 10.2.

In most of North America, the phase-to-phase voltage is 208V (this is referred to as single-phase 208V because a load across the two phases sees a single waveform) and the phase-to-neutral voltage is 120V. In some commercial buildings the phase-to-phase voltage is 480V and the phase-to-neutral voltage is 277V. According to the NEC, the system must be grounded if it is between 50 and 1000 volts, which, for our applications, it is. The green grounding wire is actually the fifth wire, but it is not called a five-wire system because the grounding wire is considered part of the grounding system.

120/208V Wye

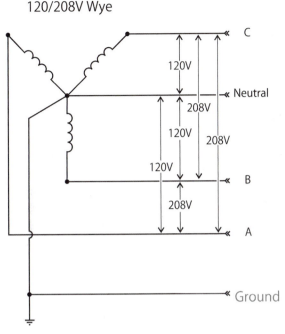

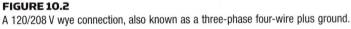

FIGURE 10.2
A 120/208 V wye connection, also known as a three-phase four-wire plus ground.

In many parts of Europe and some parts of Australia, the three-phase four-wire earthed neutral star connected system is commonly used. All countries belonging to the European Union have agreed to comply with CENELEC Harmonization Document HD 472 S1:1998, which standardizes the single-phase voltage to 230V +10%/−6% (216.2 − 253V). The nominal phase-to-phase voltage is 398.4V (sometimes indicated as 400V) and the phase-to-neutral voltage is 230V. Note that the vast majority of equipment used in Europe operates at the single-phase voltage, although there are some electric chain hoists that operate at 400 volts three-phase. Some equipment in North America operates at the phase-to-phase voltage to lower the current, and some equipment operates at the phase-to-neutral voltage. Generally speaking, if a load would draw above about 16 amps at 120V, then it is a good candidate for 208V operation.

The three-phase four-wire earthed neutral star configuration is also used extensively in the UK and Australia, but the phase-to-phase voltage is usually 415.7V and the phase-to-neutral voltage is 240V. Although both of these countries have agreed to comply with CENELEC Harmonization Document HD 472 S1:1998, they did not have to change the actual distribution voltage because 240V falls within the allowable limits of 230V +10%/–6%.

In Mexico and parts of the Middle East, South America, and Russia, a three-phase four-wire wye or star connected system is also used, but the phase-to-phase voltage is 220V and the phase-to-neutral voltage is 127V.

The differences in voltage and frequency used around the world are due to where and when their power distribution systems were developed, and the desire to standardize them has narrowed their range. The earliest systems were created independently in New York, London, Berlin, and Paris. Tesla, who was working as a consultant to the Westinghouse Electric and Manufacturing Company, was instrumental in the selection of 60 Hz as the frequency of alternating current in North America. Westinghouse engineers had designed all of their equipment to operate at 133 Hz, but they grudgingly gave in to Tesla, who insisted that 60 Hz was the ideal frequency for power generation, transmission, and equipment operation.

In Europe, one of the leading proponents of the emerging electrical technology at the time was Emil Rathenau. With the help of financiers, he bought the rights of manufacture of Edison's patents in Germany and subsequently started a company called Allgemeine Elektricitäts-Gesellschaft (AEG). They were successful in demonstrating long-distance delivery of electricity at 50 Hz. Once they demonstrated it, they stayed with that frequency. Some people believe that 50 Hz was chosen over 60 Hz because it's an easier number to deal with in the metric system.

The reasons for using 120V in North America and 230V in Europe involve geography as well. Edison chose 110 volts as a compromise between light output and filament life. The voltage had to be high enough to produce enough current, and thus enough light, to compete with the dominant illumination of the time, which was the gas lamp. But the current had to be low enough to allow his lamp filaments to last a reasonable amount of time. Across the Atlantic, Berlin Electric Works, a subsidiary of AEG, switched from 110V to 220V in order to double their capacity to deliver power without increasing their infrastructure. The idea spread throughout Europe but not to the United States.

Today, there are more than a dozen different wiring schemes for delivering electrical power to consumers around the world. The most common voltages are 100/200V in Japan and Korea; 120/208V or 120/220V in North America, much of South America, and places that were heavily influenced by the United States, such as Guam and the Philippines; 220V in China; 230V in most of Europe; and 240V in the United Kingdom, Australia, much of Africa, and places that were heavily influenced by the British, such as India.

VECTORIALLY SUMMING VOLTAGES

At first glance, it might appear that the phase-to-phase voltage should be twice the phase-to-neutral voltage in a three-phase four-wire plus ground system because the phase-to-phase voltage is measured across two phases. But in a three-phase system, the phase-to-phase voltage is 1.732 times the phase-to-neutral voltage. That's because the two phase voltages are 120° apart, and the phase-to-phase voltage is the vectorial difference between the two phase-to-neutral voltages, not the sum of their magnitudes.

To illustrate, look at Figure 10.3. It shows a vectorial representation of phase A (OA), phase B (OB), and the vectorial difference between the two (AB), which is the phase-to-phase voltage. Both phase A and phase B originate at the common node O, but phase B is 120° behind phase A (assuming a counterclockwise orientation). The reason that the phase-to-phase voltage is the difference and not the sum is that it's measured from the head of OA to the head of OB. If we trace the path from the head of OA through the common node to the head of OB, then we can see that we're traveling in the opposite direction of OA and in the positive direction of OB. Therefore, we are adding the negative of OA, which is the same as subtracting OA from OB.

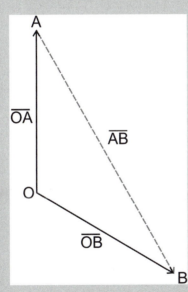

FIGURE 10.3
The vectorial sum of the phase-to-neutral voltage of two phases in a three-phase system.

To calculate the magnitude of AB, we can draw a perpendicular line from the midpoint of AB to O, as shown in Figure 10.4.

This line bisects AB (cuts it in half) and creates two right triangles. Note that the angle between OA and OB, which is 120°, is also bisected by the perpendicular line, so we

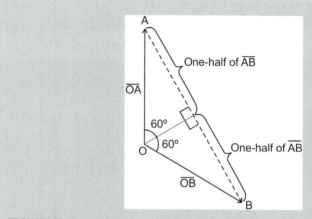

FIGURE 10.4
By drawing a perpendicular line from the midpoint of vector AB to O, we can create two right triangles and calculate the magnitude of AB.

know that each of the two angles is 60°. Looking at one of the right triangles, we now know the measure of one angle and one side, so we can calculate the length of one-half of AB by using the formula for the sine of an angle.

$$\sin\theta = \text{opposite side} \div \text{hypotenuse},$$

where the hypotenuse (the side opposite the right angle in a right triangle) is OA or OB, depending on which right triangle we're dealing with. (Let's choose OA.)

$$\sin 60° = \text{one-half of AB} \div \text{OA}$$

By multiplying both sides of this equation by OA, we get

$$\text{OA} \times \sin 60° = \text{one-half of AB}$$

Now if we use a calculator or lookup table to find the sin of 60° and multiply both sides of the equation by 2, we get

$$\text{OA}\,(2 \times 0.866) = \text{AB}$$

or

$$\text{AB} = \text{OA} \times 1.732$$

Remember that AB is the phase-to-phase voltage and OA is the phase-to-neutral voltage. To check our work, let's calculate the phase-to-phase voltage in a three-phase four-wire wye or star connected system using the formula above if the phase-to-neutral voltage is 120 volts.

$$V_{AB} = V_{OA} \times 1.732$$

$$V_{AB} = 120 \times 1.732 = 207.85 \text{ volts}$$

THREE-PHASE FOUR-WIRE DELTA (HIGH LEG DELTA)

In North America and many parts of the Caribbean and South America, the three-phase four-wire plus ground delta configuration is used almost exclusively to distribute power in commercial buildings, where most of the loads are 240V or 480V, and a small number of 120V loads are used. The neutral is tapped in the center of one of the phase windings and grounded at the service. Note that the voltage from phase B to ground is higher than any of the other two phases to ground. Phase B is known as the high leg and it is must be orange in color. A switchboard or panel with a three-phase four-wire delta system where the midpoint of one phase is grounded must be marked: "Caution _____ Phase Has _____ Volts to Ground." The name delta comes from the shape of the configuration, which resembles the Greek letter Δ (delta).

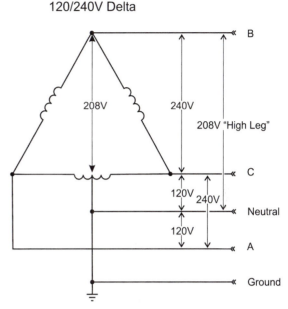

120/240V Delta

FIGURE 10.5
Three-phase four-wire delta connection with one phase winding grounded at the midpoint. Phase B is known as the high leg and it must be orange in color.

137

Where this configuration is used, the phase-to-phase voltage is typically 240V, the voltage from phase A to neutral or phase C to neutral is 120V, and the voltage from phase B to netraul is 208V. Note that, unlike the three-phase four-wire wye or star configuration, the voltage from phase A to phase B is the sum of the voltage from phase A to neutral and the voltage from phase B to neutral. That's because these voltages are measured across the same phase winding and they are in phase with each other.

SINGLE-PHASE THREE-WIRE EARTHED MIDPOINT

In residential areas and some older commercial areas in North America (excluding Mexico), a three-phase delta system is distributed to individual consumers by routing two of the phase conductors plus the neutral conductor to the building. The customer then has a single-phase three-

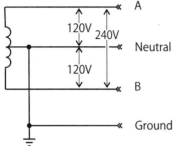

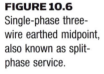

FIGURE 10.6
Single-phase three-wire earthed midpoint, also known as split-phase service.

wire earthed midpoint system, also known as a split-phase service. The two phases are fed from a single winding of a distribution transformer, and the neutral is tapped at the center of the phase winding as shown in Figure 10.6. Since each customer has a distribution transformer, it is a separately derived system.

The utility can easily provide this service by running a three-phase delta transmission system through a neighborhood and then tapping into it with a single-phase center-tapped distribution transformer and running the two phases and the neutral to the building. As long as each distribution transformer is distributed equally between the three phases, the system is in balance.

In the parts of the world where this configuration is common, the typical voltages are 240V phase-to-phase and 120V phase-to-neutral.

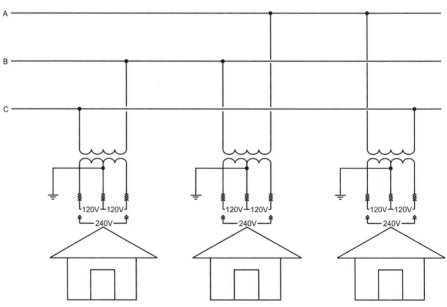

FIGURE 10.7
Typical three-phase delta distribution showing single-phase center-tapped feeder transformers feeding individual consumers. Each feeder transformer is connected to two different phases of the three-phase delta system to evenly distribute the load.

SINGLE-PHASE THREE-WIRE EARTHED END OF PHASE

A variation of the single-phase three-wire system in which the neutral wire is tapped at the end of the phase winding instead of the center is used in many parts of the world, including most of Europe, South America, China, and Australia. The wiring scheme is shown in Figure 10.8.

The exact voltage depends on the country in question, but it typically is 220V, 230V, or 240V.

220-240V

A

Neutral

Ground

FIGURE 10.8
Single-phase three-wire earthed end of phase system as used throughout Europe, Asia, Australia, and South America.

COLOR CODES

The conductors in a power distribution system are usually color coded according to the standard in use in the country in which the system is built, installed, or used. In the United States the only color codes designated by the NEC are white for neutral and green, green with yellow stripes, or bare copper wire for the grounding wire. There are no designated colors for the phase conductors, but standard practice is for phase A to be black, phase B to be red, and phase C to be blue. The sole exception is that the high-leg conductor of a 120/240 four-wire delta-connected system is orange. The entertainment production industry is fairly rigid in practice, and most every three-phase four-wire plus ground system follows the unwritten standard of black, red, blue, white, and green for phase A, phase B, phase C, neutral, and the grounding wire, respectively.

Most every other country follows a standard that spells out the color for each phase conductor, neutral, and the grounding wire or protective earth. But the codes are complicated by the fact that they have been changed in Europe and Australia in the last few years, and there are still many installations using the former standards. A brief overview of the color codes and standard practice in selected countries is shown in Figure 10.9.

139

	Australia	Canada	China	Europe since 2007; UK since 2004	Europe before 2007	United States
Phase A	Red	Red	Yellow	Brown	Brown or Black	Black
Phase B	White	Black	Green	Black	Brown or Black	Red
Phase C	Blue	Blue	Red	Grey	Brown or Black	Blue
Neutral	Black	White	Light Blue	Blue	Blue	White
Grounding wire or protective earth	Green/yellow striped	Green or bare copper	Green/yellow striped	Green/Yellow Striped	Green/yellow striped	Green, green/yellow striped, or bare copper

FIGURE 10.9

Electrical wiring color codes for several countries. The only color codes that are mandated by the NEC in the United States are the colors for neutral and the grounding wire. The other colors are standard practice but are not required by the NEC.

BALANCING THREE-PHASE LOADS

In a single-phase AC system, the neutral conductor is the return path for the current. It completes the path from the phase conductor through the load and back to the mains supply panel. But in a single-phase three-wire earthed midpoint system or a three-phase four-wire plus ground wye or star system where the load is linear and is balanced among all of the phases, the currents sum in the neutral and cancel each other out. As a result, the effective current in the neutral in these systems is zero, pro-

vided the load is balanced between each of the phases and it draws in a linear fashion.

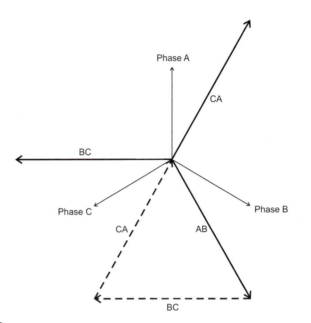

FIGURE 10.10
In a balanced three-phase load, the currents in the three phases vectorially add to zero. As a result, no current flows in the neutral conductor of a balanced three-phase four-wire plus ground wye or star connected system. Here, the light lines are the three phase-to-neutral currents, the heavy solid lines are the three phase-to-phase currents, and the dashed lines show the vectorial sum of the three phase-to-phase currents, which is zero.

A linear load is one that outputs the same waveform as the input. An incandescent lamp is an example of a linear load, and a forward-phase dimmer is an example of a non-linear load. A forward-phase dimmer, among other non-linear loads, distorts the voltage waveform and as a result causes current to flow in the neutral of a three-phase four-wire plus ground system regardless of how the load is distributed among the phases.

In the entertainment production industry, it is virtually impossible to perfectly balance a three-phase system because the load is constantly changing from cue to cue. Still, it is a good idea to start with a balanced load, assuming 100% intensity for every connected fixture. In the worst case scenario, an unbalanced load will cause the same amount of current flowing through a single phase winding to flow through the neutral (assuming a linear sinusoidal load such as a lighting system without electronic dimming).

UNDERSTANDING POWER DISTRIBUTION SYSTEMS

10.1 In a three-phase four-wire plus ground wye or star connected system, to which conductors does the common node connect?

10.2 In a 208/120V three-phase four-wire plus ground system, how do you get 208 volts? How do you get 120 volts?

10.3 If a country complies with CENELEC Harmonization Document HD 472 S1:1998, what is the allowable range of single-phase voltage?

10.4 The text box on page 135 illustrates how the resultant of the vector sum of phase A and phase B in a three-phase system is another vector with a magnitude equal to 1.732 times the magnitude of the phase-to-neutral voltage. If the phase-to-neutral voltage in a three-phase system is 230V, what is the magnitude of the phase-to-phase voltage?

10.5 Referring to Figure 10.3 on page 135, what is the phase angle of the phase-to-phase voltage? (Hint: It's the phase angle of the vector AB.)

10.6 Using vectors is one way to illustrate how two out-of-phase voltages react with each other and why we don't simply add their magnitudes. Another way of illustrating this principle is to use a spreadsheet to create two voltage sinewaves that are 120° out of phase with each other, and then subtract one from the other (because of the way the vectors are oriented; see Figure 10.3). By selecting a number of sample points we can show the resulting phase-to-phase voltage in a graph. Follow the instructions below to create your own spreadsheet and illustrations.

a. Open a new file in Microsoft Excel.

b. Type the number "0" in cell A1.

c.   Click and drag the fill handle in the bottom right-hand corner of cell A1 down to cell A361.

d.   In the toolbar, click on Edit, then Fill, then Series.

e.   Fill in these values in the window: Series in Columns; Step value 1; Stop value 360; Type – Linear. It should fill in the values from 0 to 360 in cells A1 through A361. This column now represents the phase angle.

f.   In cell B1, type the following formula without the quotes or the period at the end: "= 169.73*SIN (RADIANS(A1))." This represents the instantaneous voltage of phase A at the phase angle in cell A1 (the peak voltage times the sin of A1 in degrees).

g.   Click and drag the fill handle in the bottom right-hand corner of cell B1 down to cell B361. It should fill in the instantaneous voltage in each cell using the phase angle in the cell to the left. You have now created a sinewave showing 361 sample points from 0° to 360°. To illustrate it in a chart, make sure all the cells from B1 to B361 are highlighted, then click on Insert in the toolbar, then Chart, and for Chart type, click on Line. Now click on Finish, and Excel should open a new window with a line chart of a sinewave, as shown in Figure 10.11.

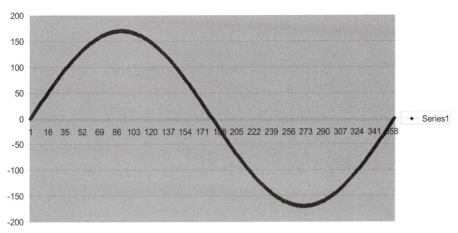

FIGURE 10.11
Phase A voltage sinewave created in Excel.

h.   In cell C1, type the following formula without the quotes or the period at the end: "=169.73*SIN(RADIANS(A1-120))." This represents the instantaneous voltage of phase B with a phase angle 120° behind the phase angle of phase A.

i.   Click and drag the fill handle in the bottom right-hand corner of cell C1 down to cell C361. It should fill in the instantaneous voltage of phase B in each cell.

j.   Make sure all the cells from C1 to C361 are highlighted, then click on Insert in the toolbar, then Chart, and for Chart type, click on Line. Now click on Finish, and Excel should open a new window with a line chart of a sine-wave that is 120° out of phase with phase A.

k.   In cell D1, type the following formula without the quotes or the period at the end: "= B1-C1." This represents the instantaneous phase-to-phase voltage. Remember, we're subtracting rather than adding because of the orientation of the windings. Referring to Figure 10.3, if you trace a path through the windings from A to B, you'll see that you're going from the head of one winding to the common point, then from the common point to the head of the second winding; one is oriented one direction and the other in the opposite direction.

l.   Click and drag the fill handle in the bottom right-hand corner of cell D1 down to cell D361. It should fill in the instantaneous phase-to-phase voltage in each cell.

m.   Make sure all the cells from D1 to D361 are highlighted, then click on Insert in the toolbar, then Chart, and for Chart type, click on Line. Now click on Finish, and Excel should open a new window with a line chart of a sinewave showing the phase-to-phase voltage.

n.   Look in column D for the peak instantaneous voltage. If you did this exercise correctly, then it should be 293.981 volts and it should appear in cell D62.

o.   Since this is the peak voltage, to calculate the RMS phase-to-phase voltage, multiply the peak voltage by 0.707. The result is 207.84 volts.

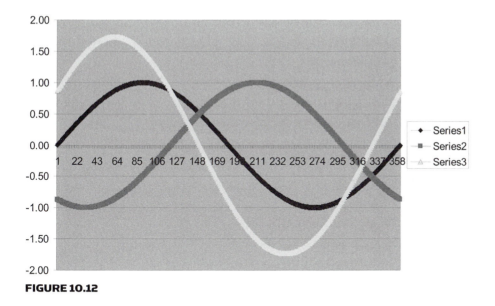

FIGURE 10.12

p. To see the relationship between all three sinewaves, click on the column heading B and drag it to the column heading D. It should highlight all three columns from B to D.

q. Click on Insert in the toolbar, then Chart. Excel should open a new window. Now click on Chart type: Line, then Finish. Excel should open a new window with a chart that looks like the illustration in Figure 10.12. The blue line is phase A, the magenta line is phase B, and the yellow line is the phase-to-phase voltage. Note that the phase-to-phase voltage starts at 330°.

10.7 If a three-phase four-wire plus ground system has a phase-to-phase voltage of 200 volts at 50 Hz, what is the voltage from phase A to ground?

10.8 In a three-phase four-wire plus ground wye or star system, the phase-to-phase voltage is 1.732 times the phase-to-neutral voltage. What is the phase-to-phase voltage compared to the phase-to-neutral voltage in a three-phase high leg delta system? Why?

10.9 What is the difference between a three-phase four-wire plus ground delta system and a single-phase three-wire plus ground system?

10.10 What is the difference between a single-phase three-wire plus ground earthed midpoint system and a single-phase three-wire earthed end of phase system?

10.11 Are color codes for power distribution systems universal?

10.12 In the United States, what are the phase colors in a three-phase system?

10.13 In Europe, what are the colors of the circuit protective conductor and the neutral?

10.14 How much current flows through the neutral in a balanced three-phase four-wire plus ground star or wye system with a linear load?

10.15 How much current flows through the neutral in a balanced single-phase three-wire earthed midpoint system?

CHAPTER 11
Dimming Systems

"I invented electronic dimming in 1939 and everybody
laughed ... This whole idea was looked down upon
with much disdain. The idea of using inverse polarized
rectifiers was a new idea way back then."

**George Izenour, professor emeritus of theatre design and
technology and director emeritus of the electro-mechanical
laboratory of the Yale University School of Drama, quoted from *A
Spin Around Moving Lights* by Raymond A. Kent**

Electronic dimming was one of the most important inventions in the
history of theatre and entertainment production. With few exceptions, no
serious lighting designer would think of designing a lighting rig without
using dimming.* Unless the rig is completely automated or uses digital
lighting, the dimmers will be either conventional phase-control dimmers
or sinewave dimmers. Regardless of the choice of technology, there are
consequences for power distribution for each type of dimming system.

PHASE-CONTROL DIMMING

Conventional dimmers use an electronic switching device to turn the
voltage on 120 times every second in a 60-Hz system or 100 times every
second in a 50-Hz system, varying the length of time the voltage is held

---

*In 2004, Todd Rundgren toured with a lighting rig that had no conventional lights, only
LEDs, with the sole exception of two followspots. There were no conventional dimmers,
only LED power supplies with built-in dimming. The lighting designer, Alex Skowron, is
by every measure a serious lighting designer.

FIGURE 11.1
Typical portable
dimmer rack. (Photo
courtesy of LSC, www
.lsclighting.com.au.)

on compared to the length of time it is held off. The duration of the on cycle, from 0 to 100%, determines the dimming level. This method of controlling the dimming level by varying the duty cycle of the voltage wave-form is called phase-control dimming.

In Figure 11.2, the switch at the bottom of the illustration turns on and off twice during each cycle: it turns off at 0° and on at 45°, then it turns off again at 180° and on again at 225°. It repeats this sequence for every cycle of the voltage sinewave until the dimming level changes. Note that the switch-ing in the negative half cycle mirrors that of the positive half cycle. Otherwise, the voltage waveform will generate a DC offset, which can damage the components in the circuit.

The switching device is either a triac or a silicon controlled rectifier (SCR). Both are solid-state switches that are controlled by a low-voltage control signal. The control signal originates at the lighting console, which outputs a low-voltage digital signal that is sent to the dimmer. The processor in the dimmer takes the output of the console and translates it to a timing signal that is referenced to the zero crossing of the AC voltage. That timing signal turns the switch on at precisely the right phase angle relative to the sinewave. The voltage is turned on, and when the phase angle reaches 180° in the positive half cycle or 360° in the negative half cycle, the voltage goes back to zero and stays off until the next switching cycle. The resulting modified voltage waveform corresponds to a particular dimming level.

A triac is a bi-directional switch, meaning it can conduct current in both the positive and negative directions. On the other hand, an SCR is a uni-directional switch; it can conduct in only one direction. In order to conduct for the full voltage cycle, dimmers that use SCRs have two devices connected in parallel and inverted in polarity. That way, the first conducts during the positive half cycle while the second is off, and the second conducts during the negative half cycle while the first is off. SCRs are more robust than triacs, and therefore dimmers with SCRs tend to be more robust than dimmers with triacs. On the other hand, SCRs are more expensive than triacs.

When the voltage is switched on during the middle of the cycle, the current rises very quickly to catch up with the voltage. As a result, it produces a current spike and overshoots the level where it should be.

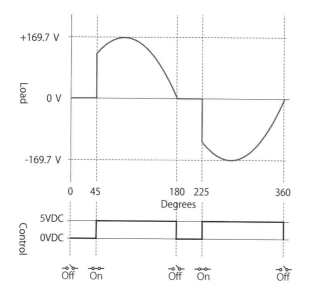

FIGURE 11.2
Modified voltage waveform showing the switching action of a conventional phase-control dimmer. The control signal at the bottom of the illustration turns a switch on and off at precisely the right time to create the right dimming level.

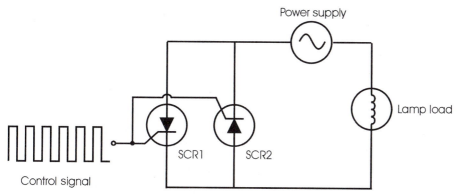

FIGURE 11.3
Conventional phase-control dimming circuit showing two SCRs (SCR1 and SCR2) connected in inverse parallel fashion. The control signal regulates the duty cycle of the current flow, thus dimming the lamp.

The sharp edges of the modified waveform cause mechanical vibration of the filament, which produces an audible frequency referred to as filament sing. The frequency and amplitude are dependent upon the dimmer level and the resonant frequency of the filament. It's loudest when the dimming level is about half.

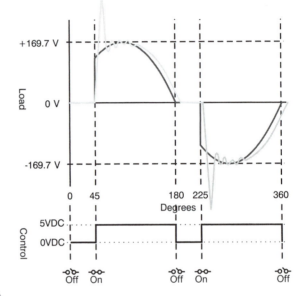

FIGURE 11.4
In a conventional phase-control dimmer, the voltage turns on in the middle of the cycle and the current rises quickly to try to catch up. As a result, it overshoots its target, finally settling down to its correct level.

To help mitigate this problem, a choke is placed in series with the load to limit the flow of current. A choke is nothing more than an inductor, so conventional dimmers present an inductive load to the supply. The larger the choke, the greater the inductive reactance and the more it slows down the current. The rise time is a measure of the effectiveness of the choke; it's measured in microseconds, or μsec (10^{-6} seconds). The greater the rise time, the less mechanical vibration the filament experiences. In North America, inexpensive dimmers can have a rise time of about 80 μsec or less, and standard dimmers usually have a rise time of about 350 μsec. Improved performance dimmers have a rise time of about 500 μsec, and high-rise time dimmers have a rise time of up to 800 μsec. Of course, bigger chokes cost more to produce; therefore, high-rise dimmers are sold at a premium. They're also heavier because they have more copper windings.

FIGURE 11.5
Dimmer modules showing chokes. On the left is a single-channel dimmer module with 800-μsec chokes; on the right is a dual-channel dimmer module with 350-μsec chokes. Note the difference in size between the high-rise choke and the standard choke. (Photo courtesy of Leviton.)

REVERSE PHASE-CONTROL DIMMING

Conventional phase-control dimmers use switching devices like triacs or SCRs that can turn the voltage on at any time during the voltage cycle, but they can turn off only at the zero-crossing point when there is no current flowing. So, while they're good at conventional phase-control — switching on during the voltage cycle — they can't be used for reverse phase-control dimming — switching the voltage off during the voltage cycle. But there are devices that can be used for that purpose.

An insulated gate bipolar transistor, or IGBT, is a type of switching transistor that can handle large currents. It can be turned on or off at any time during the voltage cycle, hence it can be used for reverse phase-control dimming. Reverse phase-control dimming is similar to forward phase-control dimming except the switch is on at the beginning of the voltage cycle and it turns off at some point during the voltage cycle. The voltage is turned off twice during each voltage cycle: once during the positive half cycle and once during the negative half cycle. Just as with forward phase-control dimming, the two half cycles have to mirror each other or a DC offset will be produced, possibly damaging circuit components. It does so by turning off the voltage at two points separated by 180°. For example, if the positive half cycle is switched off at 60°, then the negative half cycle is switched off at 240°.

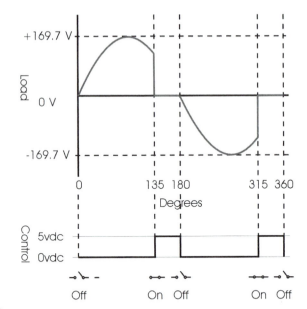

FIGURE 11.6
Reverse phase-control dimming showing the voltage waveform being turned off at 135° and turned on at 180°, then turned off again at 315° and back on at 360°.

Because the voltage is switched off during the voltage cycle instead of being switched on, there is no current spike, no overshoot, and no need to use chokes to control the rise time. So reverse phase-control dimmers are lighter in weight and less inductive. But IGBTs and similar high-current switching transistors are more expensive than SCRs or triacs, so reverse phase-control dimmers are typically more expensive than conventional dimmers.

THIRD-ORDER HARMONICS

Much like atoms are the building blocks of the universe, sinewaves are the building blocks for all other waveforms. If we took a series of sinewaves with different frequencies and amplitudes and added them all together, we would get another waveform that is completely different than a sinewave. If we were clever enough, we could carefully select the right frequencies and amplitudes in order to create any waveform we wanted to build.

By the same token, we could take any other waveform, be it a square wave, a sawtooth wave, or any random periodic function, and deconstruct it into a series of sinewaves with frequencies that are multiples of the fundamental frequency. The frequency of the original waveform is the fundamental frequency, and whole number multiples of that frequency are called harmonics. For example, if the fundamental frequency is 50 Hz, the second harmonic is 100 Hz, the third is 150 Hz, and so on.

By way of illustration, we can add a series of sinewaves in a spreadsheet and plot the results. For the sake of brevity, we'll add only the first three sinewaves in a series of odd-numbered harmonics, each with an amplitude that is half of the previous one. Figure 11.7 shows the results taken from an Excel chart in which these three sinewaves in the series were summed. The result is a complex waveform approaching that of a square wave.

Just as sinewaves can be added together to create complex waveforms, every complex waveform can be broken down into a series of pure sinewaves. The only waveform that does not have harmonics is a pure sinewave.

153

Fundamental
frequency

3 x Fundamental
frequency

5 x Fundamental
frequency

Complex waveform

FIGURE 11.7
The complex waveform shown on the right was created by adding pure sinewaves that are odd multiples of the fundamental frequency with half of the amplitude of the previous harmonic. If we were to add more sinewaves in the series of odd multiples and decreasing amplitude, the resulting waveform would more closely resemble a square wave.

The reason that sinewave synthesis and analysis are important to us is that phase-control dimming takes a voltage sinewave and chops it up, creating a complex waveform. In the process, it produces harmonics that sum in the neutral conductor. In a three-phase balanced system, the fundamentals cancel each other out because they are 120° out of phase with each other. Second-order harmonics are twice the frequency of the fundamental and, as a result, are 240° out of phase with each other. Third-order harmonics, also known as triplens, are three times the frequency of the fundamental and are 360° out of phase with each other, which is the same as 0° degrees out of phase, or completely in phase with each other. When they sum in the neutral, they are in phase and reinforce each other, causing large currents to flow.

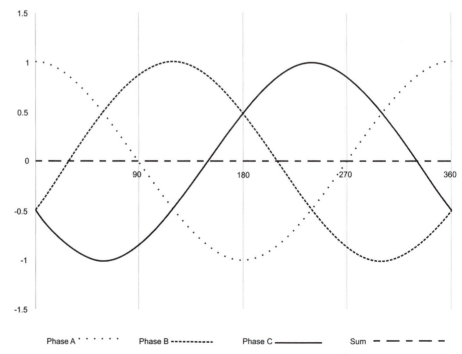

FIGURE 11.8
The three phase currents in a balanced three-phase system cancel each other in the neutral conductor, provided they are pure sinewaves. This diagram shows the fundamentals, which are 120° out of phase with each other, summing to zero.

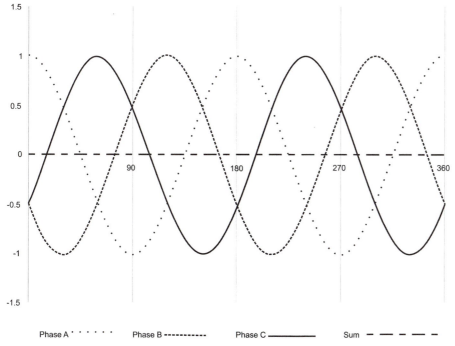

FIGURE 11.9
The secondary harmonics (twice the fundamental frequency) are 240° out of phase with each other and cancel in the neutral conductor.

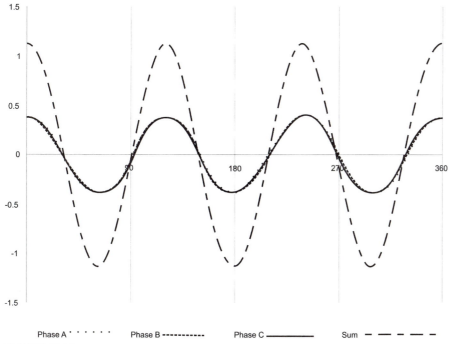

FIGURE 11.10
The third-order harmonics (three times the fundamental frequency) are in phase with each other. When they sum in the neutral conductor, they reinforce each other, possibly overloading the neutral.

As we can see by the illustration in Figure 11.10, the neutral current is three times the amplitude of the triplen currents. If the neutral is not sized correctly, it can overheat. Even if the neutral is oversized, third-order harmonics can cause nuisance tripping, overheat transformers, and pollute the power supplied to the rest of the building.

SINEWAVE DIMMING

High-current handling transistors can also be used to dim loads by using pulse-width modulation instead of phase-control. A sinewave dimmer turns the voltage on and off several thousand times during each cycle, varying the width of the voltage pulse. The output follows the voltage sinewave, but the amplitude varies according to the width of the voltage pulse. The result is that the original sine waveform is maintained and the load is dimmed according to the duty cycle of the voltage pulses. For example, when the duty cycle of each voltage pulse is 50%, the dimming level is 50%.

The switching frequency of sinewave dimmers is in the 30-kHz to 50-kHz range, although new and faster technology will allow for higher switching frequencies. The advantage of higher switching frequencies is that they can operate with smaller inductors and transformers.

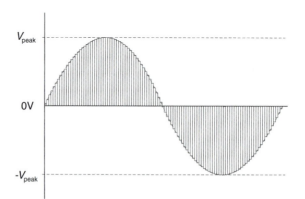

FIGURE 11.11
A sinewave dimmer varies the amplitude of a sinewave by pulse-width modulation. A transistor switches the voltage on and off several thousand times during each voltage cycle. The duration of the voltage pulse determines the voltage level.

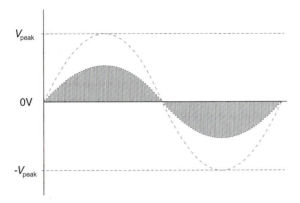

FIGURE 11.12
A sinewave dimmer waveform illustrating 50% pulse-width and the resulting voltage amplitude.

Sinewave dimmers are considered linear loads, meaning that they draw current in a linear fashion; if the voltage input is a sinewave, then the current is drawn in a sinusoidal waveform. If the voltage input is something other than a sinewave, the output would have the same waveform but the amplitude would vary with the pulse width. The advantages of having a linear load are many. First of all, a sinewave dimmer produces no third-order harmonics, and by extension, they produce no overcurrent in the neutral conductor of a balanced three-phase system even when they are dimming. They also produce no filament sing, they require no chokes to control the rise time, and they are much quieter than conventional dimmers. But large current handling transistors are expensive and sinewave dimmers command a premium price.

157

FEEDER TRANSFORMERS FOR NON-LINEAR LOADS

The vast majority of entertainment lighting systems we encounter today have dimming or other non-linear loads such as the switch-mode power supplies found in many automated lights. Not all of them, however, have so many non-linear loads compared to linear loads as to warrant great concern. If you are building a permanently installed lighting system with a greater percentage of non-linear loads to linear loads, then it is worthwhile to investigate using specially built transformers to deal with the currents generated in the neutral. Two such options include K-rated transformers and harmonic mitigating transformers (HMTs).

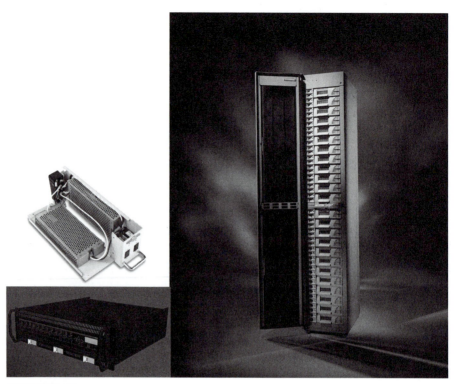

FIGURE 11.13
Strand Sinewave Dimmer Module (upper left), Swisson XSD Sinewave Dimmer pack (bottom left), and ETC Sensor+ Sinewave Dimmer rack.

K-RATED TRANSFORMERS

A K-rated transformer is a specially constructed delta-wye transformer designed to withstand the heat and effectively manage the harmonics produced by non-linear loads. They were developed in the 1980s after the proliferation of personal computers created a surge in non-linear loads and conventional transformers began overheating and failing more often. K-rated transformers have bigger conductors, special winding geometry, heat-managing cooling ducts, bigger iron cores, and an oversized neutral terminal. In addition, the delta-wye configuration isolates the triplen harmonic currents and keeps them from propagating through the entire electrical system because they recirculate in the delta primary windings.

The K factor (factor K in Europe) is a measure of the amount of heat generated in a transformer due to the harmonic content; it is derived from a ratio of the harmonic content of a waveform compared to the overall current. The K rating of a transformer is an indication of how well it can deliver power to non-linear loads without exceeding its temperature range. The values range from 1 to 50, but manufacturers typically stick to a few standard ratings, including 4, 9, 13, 20, 30, 40, and 50. An article written by Steve Terry in the Summer 2002 issue of *Protocol Magazine* (published by ESTA, www.esta.org) called "Power Play: Considerations for Feeding Permanent Dimmer-per-Circuit Systems" addresses the issue of how to select the proper K-rated transformer for dimming applications:

> For a typical SCR phase-control dimming system, field experience in a number of installations has shown that a K-13 rating is an appropriate choice. This is not based on calculation of the dimmer system's precise harmonic content, since it is almost impossible to characterize because it is different for every possible permutation of dimmer settings and loads. Many engineers have trouble with this empirical method of K-rating, since a lot of familiar harmonic generating equipment such as variable frequency motor drives can be precisely characterized. However, field experience has validated this method.

K-rated transformers handle heat well, but they are less efficient than standard transformers and they distort the voltage under non-linear loads.

HARMONIC MITIGATING TRANSFORMERS

A harmonic mitigating transformer (HMT) is designed to reduce the impedance offered to harmonic currents due to non-linear loads. Each of the three windings in the secondary is split between two poles of a three-pole iron transformer core. The poles are arranged in a zigzag configuration so that the magnetic flux between the split windings cancel each other, thus canceling the harmonic currents. The primary can be a delta or a wye (also known as a star), and the combination is known as a delta- or wye-zigzag transformer.

The reduced impedance also increases the efficiency, decreases the operating temperature, and provides better power quality. HMTs cost more than a standard transformer, but they have a relatively quick payback.

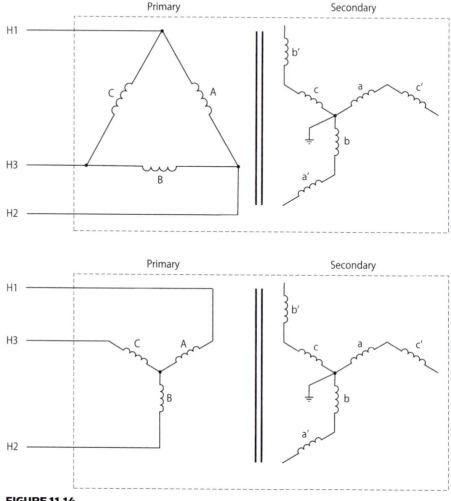

FIGURE 11.14
Delta-zigzag (top) and wye- or star-zigzag transformer (bottom). The split winding configuration is designed to present low impedance to harmonic currents by setting up the magnetic flux in a-a', b-b', and c-c' to cancel each other.

HMTs are also designed to attenuate the 5th, 7th, and 11th harmonics through phase shifting. These harmonics are byproducts of variable frequency drive circuits, but they are relatively insignificant in phase-control dimming.

HARMONIC SUPPRESSION SYSTEMS

Another way of addressing third-order harmonic currents is to use a tuned RLC (resistor-inductor-capacitor) filter to block 150-Hz or 180-Hz

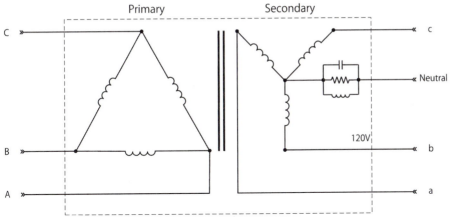

FIGURE 11.15
Harmonic suppression systems like this should not be used with dimming systems. The RLC circuit connected between the neutral conductor and the neutral terminal of the delta-wye transformer blocks third harmonic currents from circulating in the system. It also introduces voltage distortion, which can cause dimmers to operate erratically.

currents, but these harmonic suppression systems should not be used with dimming systems. By placing an RLC circuit with the right values in series between the neutral conductor and the neutral terminal of the secondary on a delta-wye transformer, the third harmonic currents present very high impedance while the currents of the fundamental frequency see none. This system effectively blocks the triplens and keeps them from circulating in the system.

The problem with using this type of harmonic suppression is that it distorts the voltage and leads to poor power quality. The voltage waveform becomes flat at the peak and begins to resemble a square wave. For many applications, such as personal computers, fax machines, and copiers, this distortion won't adversely affect their operation. But for dimming applications, it could very well cause erratic behavior including flickering and inconsistent dimming.

UNDERSTANDING DIMMING SYSTEMS

11.1   If a conventional forward phase-control dimmer turns on at 90° and off at 180°, and then turns on again at 270° and off at 360°, what is the dimming level?

161

11.2   Why does it take two SCRs to dim a load while it takes only one triac?

11.3   What is the cause of filament sing?

11.4   What is typically done to help reduce filament sing in a conventional forward-phase dimmer?

11.5   What is meant by the rise time of a dimmer?

11.6   What is a reverse phase-control dimmer? What type of switching device is used for reverse phase-control and why?

11.7   If a forward phase-control dimmer switches off at 35°, at what phase angle should it turn back on and off again to avoid creating a DC offset?

11.8   Why are reverse phase-control dimmers lighter and more expensive than forward phase-control dimmers?

11.9   What is the fundamental frequency, second harmonic frequency, and third harmonic frequency of a 120-Hz sawtooth wave?

11.10   How are sinewaves the building blocks of all other waveforms?

11.11   To better understand how sinewaves can be added to create another waveform, complete the following steps using a computer with an Excel spreadsheet. The first step is to create three sinewaves, one with the fundamental frequency, one with the second harmonic frequency (twice the fundamental frequency), and one with the third harmonic frequency (three times the fundamental frequency). Then we'll add them and chart the results.

a.   Open a new file in Microsoft Excel.

b.   Type the number "0" in cell A1.

c.   Click and drag the fill handle in the bottom right-hand corner of cell A1 down to cell A361.

d.   In the toolbar, click on Edit, then Fill, then Series.

e.   Fill in these values in the window — Series in Columns; Step value 1; Stop value 360; Type — Linear. It should fill in the values from 0 to 360 in cells A1 through A361. This column represents the phase angle.

f.   In cell B1, type the following formula without the quotes or the period at the end: "= COS(RADIANS(A1))."

g. Click and drag the fill handle in the bottom right-hand corner of cell B1 down to cell B361. It should fill in the value of the cosine for the phase angle to the left in each cell. You have now created a cosine series with 361 sample points from 0° to 360°.

h. In cell C1, type the following formula without the quotes or the period at the end: "= 0.5*COS (RADIANS(3*A1))."

i. Click and drag the fill handle in the bottom right-hand corner of cell C1 down to cell C361. It should fill in the value of the cosine for three times the frequency and half of the amplitude of the sinewave in the column to the left. This is the cosine series for the third harmonic series.

j. In cell D1, type the following formula without the quotes or the period at the end: "= 0.25*COS (RADIANS(5*A1))."

k. Click and drag the fill handle in the bottom right-hand corner of cell D1 down to cell D361. It should fill in the value of the cosine for five times the frequency and one-fourth of the cosine series in column B. This is the cosine wave for the fifth harmonic series.

l. Now that we have created the fundamental, the third harmonic series, and the fifth harmonic series, we will sum them in column E. In cell E1, type the following formula without the quotes or the period at the end: "= B1 + C1 + D1."

m. Click and drag the fill handle in the bottom right-hand corner of cell E1 down to cell E361. It should fill in the value for the sum of the three cosine waves in each cell.

n. Now highlight column E by clicking the heading in that column.

o. Click on Insert in the toolbar, then Chart. Excel should open a new window. Now click on Chart type: Line, then Finish. Excel should open a new window with a chart like that shown in Figure 11.16. The dark blue line is the fundamental, the magenta line is the third harmonic, the

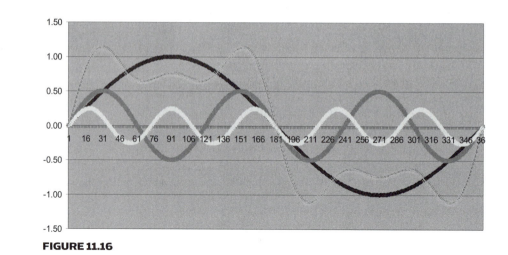

FIGURE 11.16

yellow line is the fifth harmonic, and the cyan line is the sum of the first three. Note that the new waveform was created by adding three pure cosine waveforms.

11.12 Why do triplens sum in the neutral conductor while the fundamental and second harmonics do not?

11.13 If the duty cycle of a sinewave dimmer is 25%, what is the dimming level?

11.14 What is a linear load? Is a conventional dimmer a linear load? Is a sinewave dimmer a linear load?

11.15 How does a K-rated transformer handle the harmonic currents generated by non-linear loads?

11.16 What is the meaning of the K factor or the factor K?

11.17 For a typical conventional forward phase-control dimming system, what should be the K rating of the feeder transformer?

11.18 How does a harmonic mitigating transformer (HMT) deal with harmonic currents generated by non-linear loads?

11.19 What is another name for a harmonic mitigating transformer?

11.20 How does a harmonic suppression system deal with third-order harmonics?

CHAPTER 12

Best Practices, Codes, and Regulations

"Earth meant nothing to us at the time. Bonded, possibly ... where earth and neutral were joined at the service entrance. But a third conductor for grounding? What for?"

E. H. B. "Chipmonck" Monck, referring to his days working at Capron Lighting in 1957. Chipmonck went on to become the lighting designer for Peter, Paul, and Mary, the Doors, the Byrds, the original Woodstock in 1968, the Rolling Stones, and many, many other artists and events.

Modern power distribution systems have evolved over decades and are now relatively safe, reliable, and easy to use, provided they are used with caution by qualified personnel who understand how to use them properly. Our safety record regarding electrical accidents in the industry is relatively good, although even one accident is too many. Because the electrical distribution systems we use are capable of delivering massive quantities of current, we should understand not only their components, but also how to assemble them according to the best practices and safety requirements and regulations.

This book is not intended to replace the NEC or the British wiring regs. For properly sized cable and overcurrent protection, refer to the proper codes and regulations.

TYING IN

Buildings are now required by code to have a means of disconnecting the electrical service to the building and isolating the power in order to allow maintenance, testing, fault detection, and repair. The enclosure must be listed with a recognized testing laboratory. Most modern performance spaces also have a company switch, which allows a visiting company to safely tap into the building power supply. A company switch provides a lockable disconnect that de-energizes all poles simultaneously and single-pole connector taps so your feeder cable can be safely tied in.

The company switch should be labeled with the specifications, including voltage, current, and number of phases. Connections should be made by qualified personnel, and the equipment grounding conductor should be made first and broken last, the grounded conductor (neutral) should be made second and broken second to last, and the three ungrounded conductors (phase conductors) should be made last and broken first. Under no circumstances should any connections be made or broken under load.

FIGURE 12.1
A 100A three-phase company switch with disconnect. (Photo courtesy of the Long Center for the Performing Arts, Austin, Texas.)

FIGURE 12.2
A 200A three-phase four-wire plus ground company switch. Notice that the product is UL listed and the labels indicate the proper order to connect cables and that it should be connected by qualified personnel.

Some facilities are unprepared to accommodate touring shows and offer no convenient way to tap into the building power. In these rare instances where there is no means of de-energizing the feeder panel, the only option is to use single-conductor leads with bare wire on one end and connectors on the other to tie in while the panel board is energized. *This is a dangerous maneuver and should only be considered as a last resort, and it should only be undertaken by highly qualified personnel.* (See *NFPA 70E — Working On or Near Live Parts.*) If you are unsure about how to safely do this, call in an experienced electrician who has the proper training, experience, and equipment for the job.

Power distribution systems in the live event production industry have evolved over the years through a lot of trial and error, all the while borrowing heavily from other industries like the welding and aerospace industries. Theatre has traditionally been an early adopter of lighting and electrical technology, particularly in the early days of electricity. The Great White Way, a section of Broadway between 42nd and 53rd Streets, was so nicknamed because of the Charles F. Brush arc lamps that were installed in 1880. But when concert touring came in vogue in the late 1960s and early 1970s, the concert and touring production industry took up the mantle of pioneering new technology, not necessarily out of desire but out of necessity. When the big rock concert hit the road, the techs found that they had to invent the technology and systems that would allow them to meet the challenges before them.

Before the days of manufactured and standardized systems, anyone who wanted to take their show on the road had to build their own systems from scratch. E. H. B. "Chipmonck" Monck was one of the lighting designers who helped develop the first methods and techniques for touring large systems. He had a background in theatre and ended up lighting Bob Dylan at the Newport Folk Festival, the Doors, the Byrds, Crosby, Stills, and Nash, and many, many other artists. He was instrumental in helping to build the stages and lighting systems at the first Woodstock in 1968, and he was the lighting designer/director on many early tours, including the Rolling Stones.

When Monck started touring in 1963, they commonly used the single-conductor AA asbestos insulated wire, the same wire that was used for stage lighting instruments at the time. (We now know that asbestos can cause lung disease and cancer.) Since there were no commercial stage lighting manufacturers designing and building products built for portable use back then, all of the power distribution had to be custom-made from components that were available at the time.

FIGURE 12.3

Chipmonck (center) explains to Roy Lamb (right) that he still needs to tape the five individual conductors together. They are building custom cable assemblies using AA #12AWG single-conductor cable, circa 1970.

To make matters even more difficult, the power available in the buildings at the time varied in size and configuration. In Paris in 1966, while Monck was touring with the Chamber Brothers, they encountered a four-phase six-wire system. Because of the voltage difference in Europe, they toured with three of their own 10 kVA 2:1 step-down dry type GE transformers.

FIGURE 12.4

Chipmonck (left) and David Noffsinger tie in to a 380V service in a wooden enclosure in Sweden during a stop on the Rolling Stones' STP tour circa 1970. Notice the feeder cable on the floor; it's welding cable with Tweco welding connectors.

Tweco welding connectors and welding cable were commonly used for feeder cable and connectors at the time because there were no specialized cable and connectors for portable applications. Two-wire power distribution systems (no equipment ground) were also the norm. Bob See, who started a production company called See Factor Industry, Inc. in 1970, worked in the New York City area in the 1960s and 1970s. According to See, Norman Leonard, who was the house electrician at Madison Square Garden, was responsible for introducing system grounding conductors to the touring industry. By virtue of the fact that he was a licensed electrician and he carried the license for the building, he had the power to allow or disallow shows to go on. And he insisted that any show coming in to the Garden must be properly grounded.

"Norman Leonard single-handedly changed the industry," See said. "When the circus would come in, they had to re-wire everything. He demanded that every piece of cable be three-wire. Various tours came through and they got nailed. And all of a sudden, the industry was aware that if you're going to play the Garden, you had better be 'Garden-proof.' He would not let the gear in the building unless it was three-wire. Grounding became a major league issue. He would go up and make you drop a truss and he would put a meter on it and see if you had any current coming down the truss. If he saw any current on the ground, he would make you tear the whole system apart and find out what was going on. And if you just came from a gig outdoors, all of the wire was damp. And back then, it was asbestos, so you could get current going through it. Electrically speaking, today we are safer because of him."

By the time Monck started touring with the Rolling Stones in 1969, "power was no longer an issue," he said. But power distribution systems were far from the level of sophistication they have reached today.

SINGLE-CORE CONDUCTORS, FEEDER CABLE, AND TAILS

Feeder cables, or tails in Europe, are single-core conductors that feed all the current from the source or origin to the distribution panels or boards. As such, it is important to use the correct gauge or cross-sectional area, insulation, and connector type. In permanent installations, the power distribution system is typically designed by a licensed electrical engineer and installed by licensed electricians. In portable applications, the system is typically designed by (hopefully very qualified and experienced) shop personnel and assembled on site by stage hands or touring personnel. In the United States, the NEC gives guidelines for the proper construction and operation of feeder cable in *Article 520: Theaters, Audience Areas of Motion Picture and Television Studios, Performance Areas, and Similar*

Locations. In the UK, the applicable standard is *BS 7671: Requirements for Electrical Installations*, colloquially known as "the wiring regs."

In the entertainment industry, type SC is commonly used for portable single-conductor applications like feeder cable and tails. It is listed as extra-hard usage cable and it is flexible enough to coil to a manageable size, yet it's durable enough to withstand the abuse of rough handling. It can be used indoors or out. It is jacketed with a thermoset (or rubber) outer covering and is available in sizes ranging from 6 AWG to 250 kcmil or 250,000 circular mils (millionths of an inch) and in temperature ratings of 60°C (140°F), 75°C (167°F), 90°C (194°F), or 105°C (221°). Thermoset, as the name implies, is a type of plastic that cures or hardens through the addition of heat to form a stronger, more durable compound.

As late as 1984, when the Olympics came to Los Angeles, the NEC recognized only type S or type SO cable for single-conductor feeders, and it had only been put in the code that year. Ironically, there was no such thing as single-conductor type S or type SO cable at the time because manufacturers didn't make it. Most production houses used welding cable with single pole welding or cam-type connectors. But it wasn't suited for such use because it was 90-volt, intermittent-duty cable. Manufacturers interested in capturing some of the entertainment market started making 600-volt welding cable, and most production houses on the west coast bought and used it.

But that spring, a Los Angeles County inspector red-tagged a temporary building being used for the live broadcast of the Olympics because it was powered via welding cable and terminated in cam-style connectors at the building. Soon thereafter, city officials received a letter asking for permission to use a particular brand of continuous-duty cable that was rated for 600 volts. Up until that time, the City of Los Angeles had never officially addressed the issue of acceptable feeder cable types: it had never come up, so they simply ignored it. But the letter asking permission to use this particular type of feeder cable forced the city to take action.

Their resolution was that they granted permission to use it only during the Olympics, but not afterward. They completely disallowed the use of welding cable, much to the chagrin of all of the production companies with this particular type of cable, who would have to trash it. Without the weight of the NEC behind the use of the new 600 volt feeder cable, there was no other choice. But the problem was that the NEC wouldn't write the new cable into the code unless it was UL listed for that particular purpose. In 1987, type W and type G was added to the ampacity table for feeder cable [Table 400.5 (B)], but the table didn't list ampacities for single conductors, only two- and three-conductor cables.

Also, these cables were rated for 2000 volts, they were double-jacketed, and they were very heavy. No one wanted to use them.

Over time, type W and type G cables were used as the basis to get single-conductor feeder into the ampacity table. Once that hurdle was cleared, a cable manufacturer convinced UL to list their cable, albeit not as a particular cable type, but marked "for use in accordance with Articles 520 and 530 of the NEC." This cable had blue insulation and was as flexible as welding cable. It seemed to be a success. But the issue was far from resolved.

The blue insulation on this cable was made of thermoplastic (PVC), not thermoset (rubber), as is the case for the entertainment cable we currently use. As the name implies, thermoset is set by heat, and then it stays set under the worst of conditions. Thermoplastic, on the other hand, retains its plasticity as it heats, cools, and reheats, over and over again. A cigarette would burn this cable, and the hot city streets of L.A. would melt it. The infamous blue cable that now permeated the industry had to be thrown away.

But in the meantime, a precedent was set. Over the next revision cycle of the NEC, a USITT committee with Mitch Hefter, Ken Vannice, Randy Davidson, Mike Lanni, Mike Skinner, Dick Thompson, Mark Bauserman, Steve Terry, and others wrote proposals to allow other single-conductor cables that were listed and met other necessary requirements. The result was type SC (thermoset or rubber), SCT (thermoplastic or PVC), and SCE (thermoplastic elastomer) cable. Type SC, sometimes called entertainment cable, is now the most commonly used cable for portable single-conductor applications.

Feeder cable should be sized according to the "maximum load that the switchboard is intended to control in a given situation," meaning that a dimmer rack, breaker panel, or portable power distribution unit need not be fed to its full nameplate capacity if it is not fully loaded. But the feeders must be protected by an overcurrent device with an amp rating equal to or smaller than the ampacity of the feeder cable. It's also required that tripping the feeder overcurrent protection device will not interrupt the egress or emergency lighting.

In the United States, NEC ampacity tables are used to look up the proper cable size to use for a particular application. The ampacity table for portable single-conductor cables lists the current-carrying capacity for single-conductor cable based on the temperature rating of the insulation and an ambient temperature of 30°C (86°F). There are also various de-rating factors such as running cables side by side in a raceway. If feeder cables are tied, wrapped, taped, or otherwise bound together, then their ampacity is governed by the rules for multiconductor cable (*NEC Table 520.44*).

In the United Kingdom, the appropriate cable size is calculated based on the current drawn by the load and several correction factors given in the wiring regs. The correction factors include the voltage drop due to the cable run, the ambient temperature, the number of conductors grouped together, and the temperature rating of the insulation.

If the rating of the main circuit breaker in a power distribution system is over 200 amps, then the grounding conductor should be sized according to table 250.122 in the NEC. Feeder conductors should be run together but not taped or otherwise bundled because they could overheat. They should be marked the appropriate color within 6 inches of the end of the cable (see the section titled "Color Codes" in Chapter 10).

FIGURE 12.5
Feeder cable should be color coded within 6 inches of the end of the cable.

Multiple feeder cables can be linked together for a longer run, but no more than three connector pairs can be used in the first 100 feet (30 meters). After that, one connector pair can be used for each additional 100 feet (30 meters). Feeder cable conductors can be paralleled provided that they are the exact same length and wire gauge.

Feeder cable should always be connected and disconnected in the proper sequence: grounding conductor first, grounded conductor (neutral) second, and phase conductors last to make a connection, and the reverse order to break a connection. Because of the high current running through the typical feeder cable, there is a lot of magnetic flux in the vicinity of the conductors. Care should be taken not to place excess feeder cable in a coil or it can overheat. Instead, excess cable should be wrapped in a figure-eight pattern so that the opposing magnetic flux will cancel. Also, the loops should be as

FIGURE 12.6
Excess feeder cable should be laid in a figure-eight pattern so that the opposing magnetic fields will cancel and prevent overheating of the conductors.

large as possible with the fewest number of coils as is practical in order to prevent overheating.

SINGLE-POLE CONNECTORS

The connectors used with feeder cable or tails are typically locking cam-type single-pole connectors. They should be listed by a recognized testing laboratory such as Underwriters Laboratory (UL) or ETL in the United States, or Canadian Underwriters Laboratory (CUL) in Canada. In Europe, they should bear a CE (European Conformity) mark, which means that they are certified by the manufacturer to conform to the applicable standards.

FIGURE 12.7
Single-pole locking cam-type connectors should be used with feeder cable. They should be listed with a recognized testing laboratory such as UL or ETL in the United States or CUL in Canada.

Single-pole cam-type locking connectors are manufactured under a variety of names by different manufacturers. Cam-Lok is the trade name of the single-pole cam-type locking connectors manufactured by Crouse-Hinds. Cam-type locking connectors are the de facto industry standard in North America for portable single-pole connectors.

In Europe, both Cam-Lok and equivalents are used, as well as PowerLock connectors made by Veam (formerly Litton-Veam) and Power Link connectors made by LK Connectors. PowerLock and Power Link connectors have an IP protection rating of 2X, meaning that they protect against personnel coming into contact with a live component of the connector and receiving an electric shock. They have a plastic cap over the contacts to achieve this IP rating. Cam-Loks have no such protection, but most power distribution systems using Cam-Loks have a spring-loaded safety cover on the female connectors to prevent the accidental contact with a live conductor.

FIGURE 12.8
Cam-type receptacle with safety cover to prevent accidental contact with a live conductor.

PowerLock and Power Link connectors are rated IP 67 in the mated condition, meaning that they protect against solid foreign objects with diameters of 50 millimeters or greater, such as a finger or the back of the hand, and they protect against water sprayed from all directions (with limited ingress permitted). Cam-Lok connectors are rated NEMA 3R, which means they are constructed for either indoor or outdoor use and provide a degree of protection to personnel against incidental contact with the live components and against falling dirt, rain, sleet, and snow, and they are not damaged by the external formation of ice.

FIGURE 12.9
PowerLock connectors made by Veam and Power Link connectors made by LK Connectors have a rating of IP 2X against electric shock and a mated condition IP rating of 67.

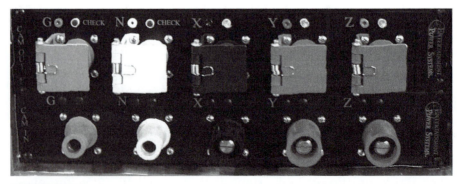

FIGURE 12.10
Panel-mount Cam-Lok connectors. Note the spring-loaded safety covers on the output connectors (top).

IP RATINGS AND NEMA RATINGS

The International Electrotechnical Commission (IEC) standard for rating an enclosure for its protection against the ingress of foreign objects and moisture is the IP rating system. In the United States, the National Electrical Manufacturers Association (NEMA) has a similar rating system for rating enclosures, called the NEMA rating. Both systems classify enclosures according to how well they protect against the elements and harsh environments.

IP CODE

The International Protection Code, or IP Code, is a two-digit code with optional suffixes for additional information about the rating. It is always preceded by the code letters IP, which stands for international protection or ingress protection.

```
                                  IP    0    0    A    H

  Code letters _____|    |    |    |

  First number indicator _____|    |    |

  Second number indicator _____|    |

  Optional additional letter indicator _____|

  Optional supplementary letter indicator _____
```

The two-digit numeric indicators are coded as follows. The first number after the code letters indicates the degree of protection against the ingress of solid objects such as dust, dirt, bird feathers, fingers, and hands. It can range from 0 to 6, and it indicates the diameter of the smallest object that can get into the enclosure:

0: Not protected
1: ≥50 mm diameter
2: ≥12.5 mm diameter
3: ≥2.5 mm diameter
4: ≥1.0 mm diameter
5: Dust protected
6: Dust tight

The second number indicates the degree of protection against the ingress of water. It can range from 0 to 8, and the highest rating is 8. The numbers are interpreted as follows:

0: Not protected
1: Protection against vertically dripping water
2: Protection against dripping water at up to a 15° angle from the vertical
3: Protection against water spray at up to a 60° angle from the vertical
4: Protection against splashing water from all directions
5: Protection against low-pressure jetting water from all directions
6: Protection against a powerful jet of water from all directions
7: Protection against temporary immersion in water less than 1 meter deep
8: Protection against continuous immersion in water at a specified depth

The first optional letter indicates the degree of protection to personnel and tools. It ranges from A to D, and the letters are interpreted as follows:

A: Protection against contact with back of hand
B: Protection against contact with finger
C: Protection against contact with tool such as a screwdriver
D: Protection against contact with wire

The supplementary optional letter indicates the degree of protection specific to four items as indicated below:
H: Protection against high-voltage apparatus
M: Enclosure was in motion during water testing
S: Enclosure was stationary during water testing
W: Protection against weather

For example, if a fixture has an IP rating of 65, then it is dust tight and rated for the protection against jetting water. The IP standard also provides for specific means of testing enclosures. A dust-tight enclosure, for example, is tested with talcum powder sifted for specific dimensions with a specific density of powder in the chamber. More information about IP ratings can be found in IEC Publication Number 60529. The document can be purchased from the IEC Web store at www.iec.ch.

IP ratings

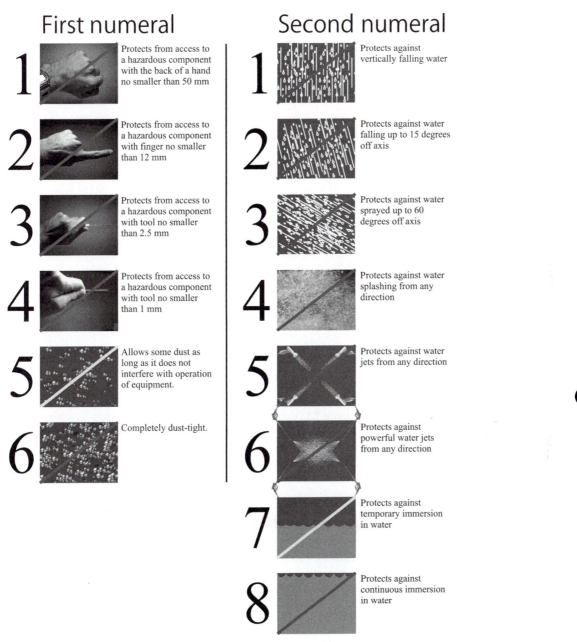

First numeral

1 — Protects from access to a hazardous component with the back of a hand no smaller than 50 mm

2 — Protects from access to a hazardous component with finger no smaller than 12 mm

3 — Protects from access to a hazardous component with tool no smaller than 2.5 mm

4 — Protects from access to a hazardous component with tool no smaller than 1 mm

5 — Allows some dust as long as it does not interfere with operation of equipment.

6 — Completely dust-tight.

Second numeral

1 — Protects against vertically falling water

2 — Protects against water falling up to 15 degrees off axis

3 — Protects against water sprayed up to 60 degrees off axis

4 — Protects against water splashing from any direction

5 — Protects against water jets from any direction

6 — Protects against powerful water jets from any direction

7 — Protects against temporary immersion in water

8 — Protects against continuous immersion in water

FIGURE 12.11

IP ratings have a two-digit code with an optional suffix describing the degree of protection of an enclosure from the elements or a harsh environment. The first digit describes the degree of protection against solid objects, and the second describes the degree of protection against the ingress of water.

NEMA RATINGS

NEMA ratings describe the application of enclosure types and the degree of protection against the environment. There are NEMA ratings for hazardous locations involving corrosive chemicals, combustibles, and gas, vapors, and dust, and there are NEMA ratings for nonhazardous locations. Since we normally avoid hazardous locations for live event production, we will only discuss the ratings for nonhazardous locations, which include NEMA types 1 through 6.

Type 1 enclosures are for indoor use and provide protection to personnel against access to hazardous parts and against the ingress of falling dirt.

Type 2 enclosures are for indoor use and provide protection to personnel against access to hazardous parts and against the ingress of falling dirt, dripping water, and light splashing of water.

Type 3 enclosures are for indoor or outdoor use and provide protection to personnel against access to hazardous parts and against the ingress of falling dirt, windblown dust, rain, sleet, snow, and the external formation of ice on the enclosure.

Type 3R enclosures are for indoor or outdoor use and provide protection to personnel against access to hazardous parts and against the ingress of falling dirt, rain, sleet, snow, and the external formation of ice on the enclosure.

Type 3S enclosures are for indoor or outdoor use and provide protection to personnel against access to hazardous parts and against the ingress of falling dirt, windblown dust, rain, sleet, snow, and protect the external mechanism(s) from becoming inoperable when laden with ice.

Type 3X enclosures are for indoor or outdoor use and provide protection to personnel against access to hazardous parts and against the ingress of falling dirt, windblown dust, rain, sleet, snow, and an additional level of protection against corrosion and the external formation of ice on the enclosure.

Type 3RX enclosures are for indoor or outdoor use and provide protection to personnel against access to hazardous parts and against the ingress of falling dirt, rain, sleet, snow, and will be undamaged by the external formation of ice on the enclosure that provides an additional level of protection against corrosion as well as protection against the external formation of ice on the enclosure.

Type 3SX enclosures are for indoor or outdoor use and provide protection to personnel against access to hazardous parts and against the ingress of falling dirt, windblown dust, rain, sleet, and snow. They also provide an additional level of protection against corrosion as well as protection against the external mechanism(s) becoming inoperable when laden with ice.

Type 4 enclosures are for indoor or outdoor use and provide protection to personnel against access to hazardous parts and against the ingress of falling dirt, windblown dust, rain, sleet, snow, splashing water, hose-directed water, and the external formation of ice on the enclosure.

Type 4X enclosures are for indoor or outdoor use and provide protection to personnel against access to hazardous parts and against the ingress of windblown dust, rain, sleet, snow, splashing water, hose-directed water, corrosion, and the external formation of ice on the enclosure.

Type 5 enclosures are for indoor use and provide protection to personnel against access to hazardous parts and against the ingress of falling dirt, settling airborne dust, lint, fibers, flying particles, dripping water, and the light splashing of water.

Type 6 enclosures are for indoor or outdoor use and provide protection to personnel against access to hazardous parts and against the ingress of falling dirt, hose-directed water, the entry of water during occasional temporary submersion at a limited depth, and the external formation of ice on the enclosure.

Type 6P enclosures are for indoor or outdoor use and provide protection to personnel against access to hazardous parts and against the ingress of falling dirt, hose-directed water, the entry of water during prolonged submersion at a limited depth, corrosion, and the external formation of ice on the enclosure.

Type 12 enclosures (without knockouts) are for indoor use and provide protection to personnel against access to hazardous parts and against the ingress of falling dirt, circulating dust, lint, fibers, flying particles, dripping water, and the light splashing of water.

Type 12K enclosures (with knockouts) are for indoor use and provide protection to personnel against access to hazardous parts and against the ingress of falling dirt, circulating dust, lint, fibers, flying particles, dripping water, and the light splashing of water.

Type 13 enclosures are for indoor use and provide protection to personnel against access to hazardous parts and against the ingress of falling dirt, circulating dust, lint, fibers, flying particles, dripping water, the light splashing of water, and the spraying, splashing, and seepage of oil and noncorrosive coolants.

For a complete description of NEMA enclosure ratings, see NEMA Standards Publication 250-2003, "Enclosures for Electrical Equipment (1000 Volts Maximum)." It is available from IHS (www.global.ihs.com).

Table 12.1	Comparison of Specific Applications of NEMA Enclosures for Indoor Nonhazardous Locations									

Provide a Degree of Protection Against the Following Conditions	Type of Enclosure									
	1*	2*	4	4X	5	6	6P	12	12K	13
Access to hazardous parts	X	X	X	X	X	X	X	X	X	X
Ingress of solid foreign objects (falling dirt)	X	X	X	X	X	X	X	X	X	X
Ingress of water (dripping and light splashing)	...	X	X	X	X	X	X	X	X	X
Ingress of solid foreign objects (circulating dust, lint, fibers, and flyings†)	...	...	X	X	...	X	X	X	X	X
Ingress of solid foreign objects (settling airborne dust, lint, fibers, and flyings†)	...	...	X	X	X	X	X	X	X	X
Ingress of water (hosedown and splashing water)	...	...	X	X	...	X	X	...	...	...
Oil and coolant seepage	...	...	...	..	...	...	...	X	X	X
Oil or coolant spraying and splashing	...	...	...	...	...	...	...	...	...	X
Corrosive agents	...	...	...	X	...	...	X	...	...	...
Ingress of water (occasional temporary submersion)	...	...	...	...	...	X	X	...	...	...
Ingress of water (occasional prolonged submersion)	...	...	...	...	...	...	X	...	...	...

*These enclosures may be ventilated.
†These fibers and flyings are nonhazardous materials and are not considered Class III type ignitable fibers or combustible flyings. For Class III type ignitable fibers or combustible flyings see the National Electrical Code, Article 500.

From NEMA 250-2003. Table courtesy of NEMA.

Table 12.2	Comparison of Specific Applications of Enclosures for Outdoor Nonhazardous Locations									

Provide a Degree of Protection Against the Following Conditions	Type of Enclosure									
	3	3X	3R*	3RX*	3S	3SX	4	4X	6	6P
Access to hazardous parts	X	X	X	X	X	X	X	X	X	X
Ingress of water (rain, snow, and sleet[†])	X	X	X	X	X	X	X	X	X	X
Sleet[‡]	...	...	...	...	X	X	...	...	...	...
Ingress of solid foreign objects (windblown dust, lint, fibers, and flyings)	X	X	...	...	X	X	X	X	X	X
Ingress of water (hosedown)	...	...	...	...	...	...	X	X	X	X
Corrosive agents	...	X	...	X	...	X	...	X	...	X
Ingress of water (occasional temporary submersion)	...	...	...	...	...	...	...	...	X	X
Ingress of water (occasional prolonged submersion)	...	...	...	...	...	...	...	...	...	X

*These enclosures may be ventilated.
[†]External operating mechanisms are not required to be operable when the enclosure is ice covered.
[‡]External operating mechanisms are operable when the enclosure is ice covered.
From NEMA 250-2003. Table courtesy of NEMA.

IP VERSUS NEMA

According to NEMA, IP ratings cannot be converted to NEMA enclosure types and vice versa. But Table 12.3 can be used to compare the two. If the box is marked, that means that the NEMA enclosure type exceeds the requirements for the IP designation in the left-hand column. The first seven rows of the IP rating (0X through 6X) indicate the degree of protection against hazardous parts and foreign objects, and the last nine rows (X0 through X8) indicate the degree of protection against the ingress of water.

Table 12.3   NEMA Enclosure Types Versus IP Ratings

	NEMA Enclosure Type								
IP Rating	1	2	3, 3X, 3S, 3SX	3R, 3RX	4, 4X	5	6	6P	12, 12K, 13
IP 0X	X	X	X	X	X	X	X	X	X
IP 1X	X	X	X	X	X	X	X	X	X
IP 2X	X	X	X	X	X	X	X	X	X
IP 3X			X		X	X	X	X	X
IP 4X			X		X	X	X	X	X
IP 5X			X		X	X	X	X	X
IP 6X					X		X	X	
IP X0	X	X	X	X	X	X	X	X	X
IP X1		X	X	X	X	X	X	X	X
IP X2		X	X	X	X	X	X	X	X
IP X3			X	X	X	X	X	X	X
IP X4			X	X	X		X	X	X
IP X5			X		X		X	X	
IP X6					X		X	X	
IP X7							X	X	
IP X8								X	

Table courtesy of NEMA.

NEUTRAL CONDUCTOR SIZING

The grounded conductor, or neutral, is the normal path for the return current, but depending on the application, it should be sized differently according to the circumstances. In a balanced three-phase system with linear loads, the phase currents cancel and the neutral current is zero. (See Figure 11.8, page 154.) Therefore, the feeder neutral is not considered a current-carrying conductor for temperature de-rating purposes.

That doesn't mean that it doesn't need to be run or that it can be smaller than the phase conductors, it just means that it doesn't contribute to the de-rating factor for multiple current-carrying conductors in a raceway. If multiple conductors are run in the same raceway, they have to be de-rated to compensate for the rise in the temperature due to the proximity of the other conductors.

In portable touring applications, the vast majority of our power distribution systems are fed with single-conductor cables in free air, so the normal de-rating factor for four conductors in a raceway does not apply; however, there are other considerations. In a multiphase system with phase-control dimmers, the neutral has to be increased in size to have an ampacity of at least 130% of the ungrounded conductors feeding the system. The reason for the increased ampacity is because, in a typical show where the lights are constantly being dimmed and scenes are changing, the load is constantly being redistributed among the phases, insuring that the system will not be balanced most of the time. And the unbalanced loading causes current to flow in the neutral. A study by the USITT determined that the worst case scenario is when one phase is loaded 100%, another is at 55%, and the third is 0%. This unbalance causes 126% of the phase current to flow in the neutral, so the NEC requires a 30% increase in ampacity of the neutral.

Another situation to consider is when a three-phase, four-wire plus ground dimmer rack is connected to a single-phase, three-wire plus ground supply. If any two of the three dimmer phases are both connected to one conductor of the single-phase supply, then there is a potential for 200% of the dimmer phase current to flow through the neutral of the dimmer rack. For example, suppose phase A and B of a 100-amp, three-phase dimmer rack are both connected to L1 of a 200-amp, single-phase, three-wire supply, and phase C of the dimmer rack is connected to L2 of the supply. If phase A and phase B are both pulling 100 amps and phase C is pulling no current, then 200 amps would flow through the neutral of the dimmer rack. (See Figure 12.12.) For that reason, dimmer racks that are not designed to be converted in the field from three-phase use to single-phase use and back must be able to carry 200% of the full current through the neutral.

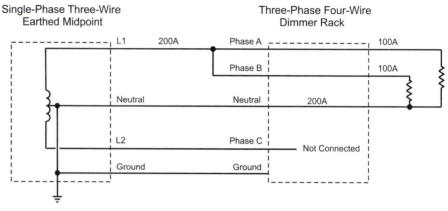

Single-Phase Three-Wire
Earthed Midpoint

Three-Phase Four-Wire
Dimmer Rack

FIGURE 12.12
The neutral conductor in a three-phase dimming system can carry 200% of the phase current if two phases are connected to a single leg of a single-phase, three-wire supply.

PORTABLE POWER DISTRIBUTION SYSTEMS

Touring road shows have to have some way of tapping into the venue power supply and distributing it to their system safely and quickly. They typically have at least one portable power distribution unit (PPD, or simply PD) that connects to the building supply and distributes power to individual branch circuits supplying each device in the system. Many of these units have become standardized to 19" rackmount dimensions housed in flight cases on heavy-duty casters for ease of transport. They typically have interchangeable modules in order to accommodate a variety of situations. The modules can be different connector types for the inputs and outputs or they can be indicators, meters, or other apparatus.

Portable PDs that are used to supply power on stage are required by code to be internally lined with noncorrosive metal and have a circuit breaker for the main input and overcurrent protection for each branch circuit or final circuit. Most have parallel output connectors or passthroughs to enable the connection of multiple PDs in a daisy-chain fashion. Some have double neutrals to better handle dimmer circuits and/or unbalanced loads. In addition, some PDs have reversed ground and neutral connectors (RGNs), meaning that the output connectors for the ground and neutral are male rather than female. This prevents the possibility of the

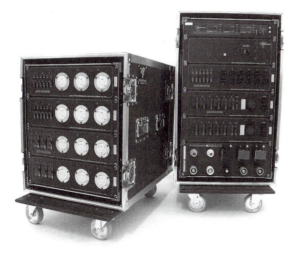

FIGURE 12.13
Portable lighting power distros. The PD on the right has digital LED phase, voltage, and load indicators (top module), main circuit breaker (second module from top), convenience outlets (third from top), two modules with Socapex multi-circuit outputs, and main inputs with cam-type locking connectors (bottom). The PD at the left shows 12 L14-30 twist-lock connectors for three-phase four-wire plus ground outputs. (Photo courtesy of Motion Labs, Inc., www.motionlabs.com.)

phase conductors being inadvertently connected to the equipment ground or circuit protective conductor, or to the grounded conductor (neutral).

Power distros should always be connected and disconnected while the feeder is de-energized and all breakers are in the off position. Once all of the cables are connected, the main breaker should be turned on before any of the branch circuits or final circuits are energized, and the proper voltage should be confirmed on the voltage monitor or with a hand-held meter using the test points on the PD. If the all phases test correctly from phase to phase and from phase to ground, then and only then should all of the branch circuit breakers or final circuit breakers be turned on. When the show is over, all lamps and amps should be doused and turned off in the proper sequence. Discharge lamps should be allowed to cool for 5 minutes with the lamps off and the fans on before shutting down the power. When they have been given sufficient time to cool, the individual branch circuit breakers should be turned off one at a time, and then the main breaker should be turned off. If there is ever a problem with a power distribution system, everything should be de-energized and every link in the system should be tested and turned on one at a time.

FIGURE 12.14
A variety of portable power distribution units. Top, left to right: Motion Labs Lighting PD, Indu Electric Tourpack Distro, Leprecon PD. Bottom, left to right: Lex Products Powerrack, PRG S-4000, CW Limited PD.

I was once touring as the lighting designer and operator when the dimmer tech turned on a company switch feeding a power distro that was fully connected with the main breaker in the on position. I was about 10 meters away from the PD when I heard a very loud popping sound, and out of the corner of my eye I saw an intense flash of bluish, red, and yellow light. I turned to look just in time to see a big puff of smoke rising over the PD. The dimmer tech turned pale and quickly shut off the company switch. Not knowing what to do next, he asked for my help.

The house electrician had left the building, and we had only a few hours until doors, so we rolled up our sleeves, gritted our teeth, and quickly went to work to resolve the problem. We disconnected every cable going to the PD and then methodically tested the system one component at a time. First we left the feeder cable tied into the company switch but left it disconnected from the PD. I held my breath, turned my face away from the disconnect switch in case it flashed, and then turned it on. Nothing happened. I turned off the company switch again. Next, we connected the feeder cable and nothing else to the PD, and we left the main circuit breaker in the off position. Again, I turned my face away from the switch and turned it on. Again, nothing happened. I turned off the company switch again. Then we turned on the main circuit breaker in the PD but left all of the branch circuits unconnected. I turned on the company switch and nothing happened. So far, so good. I turned off the company switch and the main breaker again. We then connected all of the multi-core branch circuit cable and tried the system again. When nothing happened, we turned on every branch circuit breaker.

In the end, everything held, and we determined that the short circuit that caused the problem in the first place had cleared itself. When the tour was over and the PD was returned to the shop, it was torn apart and examined. I never learned the results of the examination, but I suspect that the shop techs found either a loose piece of metal or a small rodent. Whatever it was, I'm guessing it was fried.

BRANCH CIRCUITS OR FINAL CIRCUITS

The industry has been standardized, to a degree, with regard to the use of multi-conductor cable to run branch circuits or final circuits from a portable power distribution rack or dimmer rack to the loads. Multi-core or multi-conductor cable with 19-pin circular or rectangular connectors to run six branch circuits is one of the few almost universally used pieces of gear. The cable is typically 14-conductor or 18-conductor, depending on whether the grounding conductors are bonded or run individually. Each of these branch circuits must have overcurrent protection for the individual circuit.

Many people agree that Eric Pierce, formerly of Showlites, was responsible for introducing the multi-pin Socapex connector into the United States in the early days of live event production, around 1980. The connector originally came from a French aerospace company called Amphenol.

Today, the vast majority of portable power distribution and lighting systems in North America use a 19-pin circular connector and multi-core cable to run power from the PD to the truss or other locations. In Europe you might find multi-pin connectors in circular or rectangular configurations.

FIGURE 12.15
Male 19-pin circular connector. (Photo courtesy of Creative
Stage Lighting.)

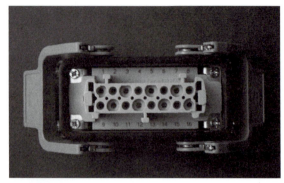

FIGURE 12.16
The Harting rectangular multi-pin connector is commonly used
in parts of Europe for distributing multiple branch circuits in a
single cable.

In 1997, the United States Institute for Theatre Technology (USITT) published a recommended practice called RP-1: Contact Function Assignments for Multi-circuit Circular Pin Connectors Used for the Distribution of Multiple Lighting Circuits. Its purpose was to help standardize the pin assignments for 19-pin and 37-pin connectors in the entertainment industry. Thirty-seven-pin connectors were used for 0–10V lighting control and 12-circuit multicables, but they have all but fallen out of favor because of their size, cost, and weight. Today, they are difficult to source from entertainment lighting suppliers.

Multi-pin connectors are available in solder- or crimp-type contacts for in-line (cable mount) or panel mount use. The pin connections are organized in two rings: an inner ring and an outer ring (plus the center pin, which is unused and therefore not connected). The pins in the outer ring are used for the ungrounded phase and grounded neutral conductors. They are arranged in adjacent pairs (ungrounded conductor, grounded conductor) and are numbered clockwise in the female connector and counterclockwise in the male connector from the user's point of view. The pins in the inner ring closest to the outer ring pin pair are used for the equipment grounding conductor (see pinout diagram in Figure 12.16). The center pin is not connected. The odd-numbers pins from 1 to 11 are the ungrounded or phase conductors, and the

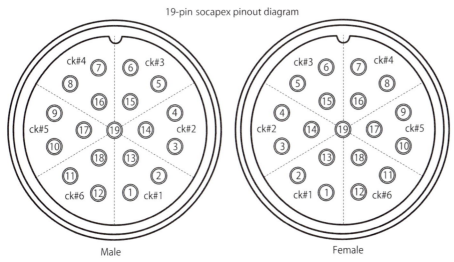

FIGURE 12.17
19-pin Socapex pinout as shown looking at the pins and sockets.

even-numbered pins 2 through 12 are the grounded or neutral conductors.

All of the equipment grounding conductors (pins 13 through 18) should be bonded to each other, and they should be made first and broken last. This is usually accomplished by the design of the connectors, which extends the length of the female pins in the inner ring so that they make first contact when the connectors are mated and last contact when they are broken apart. At least one of the equipment grounding conductors should be at least the same gauge as the largest ungrounded conductor. It is permissible to use only two equipment grounding conductors, but using all six is also permitted.

The multiconductor cable used for power distribution should be listed for extra hard usage, which includes types G, G-GC, S, SC, SCE, SCT, SE, SEO, SEOO, SO, SOO, ST, STO, STOO, and PPE. They are available in a variety of wire gauges, typically #12, #14, or #16 AWG. The ampacity of multiconductor cable and the maximum rating of the overcurrent protective circuit breaker are shown in Tables 12.5 and 12.6 for no more than one to three current-carrying conductors in a single cable.

Table 12.4	19-pin Circular Connector Six-Circuit Pinout		
Contact No.	**Function**	**Contact No.**	**Pinout**
1	Circuit #1 ungrounded conductor	11	Circuit #6 ungrounded conductor
2	Circuit #1 grounded conductor	12	Circuit #6 grounded conductor
3	Circuit #2 ungrounded conductor	13	Circuit #1 grounding conductor
4	Circuit #2 grounded conductor	14	Circuit #2 grounding conductor
5	Circuit #3 ungrounded conductor	15	Circuit #3 grounding conductor
6	Circuit #3 grounded conductor	16	Circuit #4 grounding conductor
7	Circuit #4 ungrounded conductor	17	Circuit #5 grounding conductor
8	Circuit #4 grounded conductor	18	Circuit #6 grounding conductor
9	Circuit #5 ungrounded conductor	19	Not connected
10	Circuit #5 grounded conductor		

Table 12.5	Ampacity of Listed Extra-Hard-Usage Cords and Cables with Temperature Ratings of 75°C (167°F) and 90°C (194°F)* Based on an Ambient Temperature of 30°C (86°F)		

| | Temperature Rating | | |
AWG	75°C (167° F)	90°C (194° F)	Maximum Rating of Overcurrent Device
14	24	28	15
12	32	35	20
10	41	47	25
8	57	65	35
6	77	87	45
4	101	114	60
2	133	152	80

*Ampacity shown is the ampacity for multiconductor cords and cables where only three copper conductors are current carrying as described in 400.5. If the number of current-carrying conductors in a cord or cable exceeds three and the load diversity factor is a minimum of 50%, the ampacity of each conductor shall be reduced as shown in Table 12.6.

191

Table 12.6	Ampacity De-rating Chart for Multiple Conductors in a Single Cable

Number of Conductors	Percent of Ampacity
4–6	80
7–24	70
25–42	60
43+	50

BREAKOUTS OR SPIDERS

Once power is delivered through a multiconductor cable to the vicinity of the loads, it has to be broken out to individual circuits and fed to each load. This is typically done with a breakout assembly, or spider in Europe, which is an adapter with a male multi-pin connector on one end and several individual cables terminated with female connectors on the other end.

FIGURE 12.18
19-pin connector to stage pin six-circuit breakout, or spider. (Photo courtesy of Union Connector.)

Each of the connectors should be listed two-pole three-wire connectors and the cable should be listed junior hard service cord for hard usage. The longest cord in the breakout should be no longer than 6 meters (20 feet). Also, since junior hard service cord is not durable enough to withstand being crushed by a forklift or a heavy road case, it should not be run along the ground and it should be protected by a support structure like a truss or pipe. Lastly, each branch circuit should be protected by an overcurrent device rated for no more than 20 amps.

There are a variety of two-pole three-wire connectors in use in the industry and around the world. For example, they may be terminated with Edison, stage pin, twist-lock, IEC, or Ceeform connectors.

DEVICE CONNECTORS

Around the turn of the twentieth century, Harvey Hubbell II was walking along a sidewalk in New York City as the shops were closing. He encountered a penny arcade wherein the janitor was sweeping up after closing time. Looking through the window, he noticed how the janitor had to disconnect the power cable from a game that was wired to the power supply in the wall in order to move it and sweep under it. At the time, there were no connectors, and switches were expensive, so the bare ends of the conductors were wrapped around terminal posts protruding from the wall. Each time the janitor tried to unwrap the wires, he would get a shock. The incident gave Hubbell the idea to build a connector that would mate with a receptacle in the wall. On January 2, 1912, Hubbell applied for a patent for a separable attachment plug. The two-pole two-wire connector was patented in 1913. It is essentially (and ironically) the same Edison-type connector, sans the grounding wire, that is now commonly used in North America for household applications and some commercial and theatrical applications.

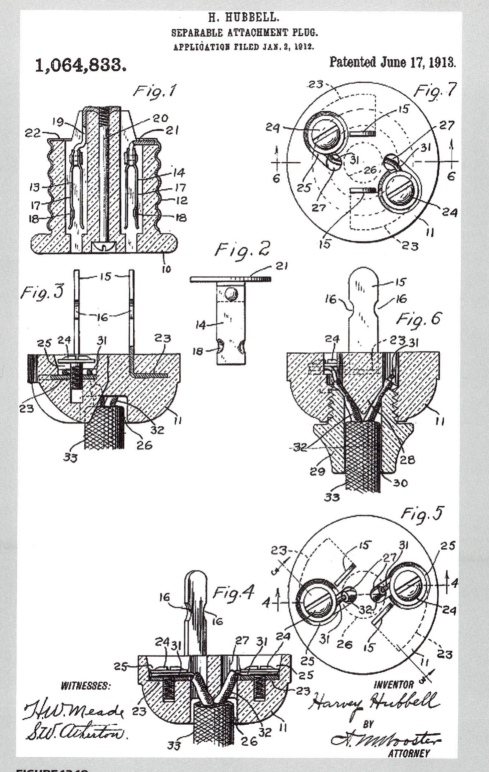

FIGURE 12.19
Harvey Hubbell's patent for a separable attachment plug, granted in 1913.

193

There are a variety of connectors used in our industry to connect devices to the mains power. Connectors often vary from country to country, and very often they vary within the same country. For example, in the United States you may find production companies using Edison, stage pin, twist-lock, or PowerCon connectors.

Connectors have both a voltage rating and a current rating. The voltage rating ensures that a connector won't arc between conductive parts, and the current rating ensures that it won't melt due to the heat generated by the current, provided it is used properly.

STAGE PIN CONNECTORS

The stage pin connector is probably the most commonly used device connector in North American theatres. These connectors are available in 120V and 250V versions for 20A, 30A, 60A, and 100A service.

FIGURE 12.20
Stage pin connectors.

One of the main advantages of the stage pin connector is that it has a lower profile and can lie flat, presenting less of a tripping hazard. The male connectors have split pins that are designed to increase the pressure applied to the female socket in order to make a better electrical connection. A pin spreader can be used to restore the proper spacing in the pins and maintain a good connection. If the pins are not properly spread, then it may cause a poor contact with the female socket and create arcing, heating, and deterioration of the pins and sockets. In that case, the pins and sockets should be cleaned with sandpaper or other abrasive material to remove the carbon buildup, which can cause further arcing, heat, and deterioration through the increased contact resistance.

NEMA CONNECTORS

In North America, electrical connectors rated up to 60 amps and 600 volts are manufactured to comply with ANSI/NEMA WD 6-2002. Of the many different NEMA classifications, only a few are commonly used in our industry. Among them are the NEMA 5-15 (also known as an Edison plug), NEMA 5-20, NEMA L5-15, NEMA L5-20, and NEMA L6-20.

The first number in the NEMA classification is a code that indicates the voltage rating and wiring configuration, and the second number indicates the current rating in amps. The letter P appended to the classification means that it's a plug, and the letter R indicates that it's a receptacle. For example, a NEMA 5-XP is a 125V, two-pole three-wire plug (the third wire is the equipment grounding wire). A NEMA 5-15P, commonly referred to as an Edison plug, is a two-pole three-wire plug rated for 125 volts and 15 amps. Until recently, it was against the NEC code to use a 5-15P connector with a 20-amp T-slot receptacle or a 5-20R, which effectively outlawed the use of Edison plugs in the theatre. That rule has since been changed. In Canada, however, a 5-20R will not accept a 5-15 plug because T-slot receptacles that allow the use of a 5-15P or a 5-20P are not used.

NEMA 6-X is rated for 250V maximum and it is a two-pole three-wire device. The more common NEMA connectors in the theatre and live event production industry are the L5-15, L5-20, L6-16, and L6-20. The prefix L means that it is a locking connector, commonly known as a twist-lock connector. These connectors have curved blades and lock by inserting the blades into the receptacle and twisting.

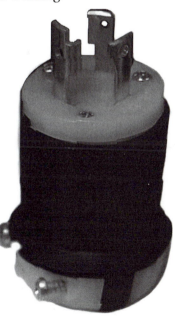

FIGURE 12.21
NEMA 5-15P 125V 15A two-pole three-wire connector, also known as the Edison plug.

FIGURE 12.22
NEMA L6-20 250V 20A twist-lock connector.

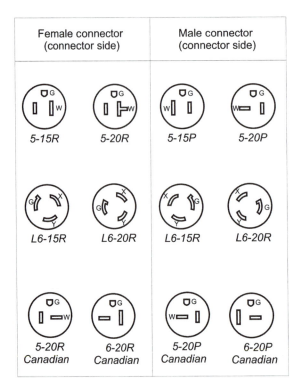

FIGURE 12.23
Common NEMA wiring device configurations in the live event production industry.

The configurations of some of the more common NEMA wiring devices used in the live event production industry are shown in Figure 12.23. The letter W indicates the location of the pole used for the grounded neutral conductor, which is whiter in color than the other poles. The letter G indicates the equipment ground. There are over a hundred more NEMA configurations, but the ones shown in Figure 12.23 are some of the most common ones that we will encounter in the theatre or in live events.

POWERCON

PowerCon is the trade name of a power connector made by Neutrik. It is a locking three-wire connector that is sometimes used for branch circuit terminations. It has no exposed conductive parts, and a keyed input and output prevents the possibility of connecting the wrong cables. The input and outputs are also color coded for easy identification. The connectors use UL- and cUL-recognized components, meaning that they have been tested and evaluated for limited, specific use. PowerCon connectors are also VDE (German testing laboratory) certified.

FIGURE 12.24
Neutrik PowerCon 32A three-wire plug (left) and receptacle.

UL LISTED OR RECOGNIZED?

Underwriters Laboratory is one of several nationally recognized testing laboratories (NRTLs) as listed by the Occupational Safety and Health Administration of the U.S. Department of Labor. Manufacturers can send a complete product to an NRTL such as UL and pay to have it tested and evaluated against recognized safety standards. If the product is found to be reasonably free of the risk of fire, electric shock, and related hazards, and it is manufactured under UL's Follow-Up Services program, then it is UL Listed. Such products always bear the UL Listing Mark, the manufacturer's name or trademark.

The UL Listing Mark has "UL" inscribed in a circle with the word "LISTED" in capital letters underneath it. If it is listed in the United States then it will have the letters "US" at the four o'clock position, and if it is listed in Canada it will have the letter "C" at the eight o'clock position.

FIGURE 12.25
The UL Mark on a product is the manufacturer's representation that the complete product has been tested and evaluated by UL to recognized safety standards and that it is reasonably free of the risk of fire, electric shock, and related hazards.

A UL Recognized product, on the other hand, is an indication that the component has been tested and evaluated to meet the criteria for limited, specific use. Such a component is intended to be used in completed products that should be submitted for testing and evaluation as a complete product to receive a UL listing. UL listings can be found on the UL Website at www.ul.com.

15-AMP PLUGS

In the UK, the 15-amp Duraplug is commonly used in the theatre for dimmed loads. It conforms to BS546, which is an obsolete standard, although its use is still permitted under the wiring regulations. The connector became popular because it was the only appliance connector without a built-in fuse, which is unnecessary in the theatre because of the overcurrent protection in dimmers. The lack of a fuse also makes it easier to troubleshoot. The 15A plug is a 250V two-pole three-wire connector.

FIGURE 12.26
The 15A Duraplug is commonly used in the theatre in the UK, even though it is manufactured to the obsolete BS546 standard.

CEE-FORM CONNECTORS

The CEE 17 connector is commonly used in the UK and other parts of Europe for hard power or non-dimmed power in the and live event production. You will find them in theatres and hire companies for a variety of applications, including automated lighting.

CEE-form connectors in general comply with IEC 60309 European Approved Wiring Devices. This standard defines heavy-duty pin and sleeve plugs and receptacles. They are explosion-proof, chemical resistant, and rated IP 44 (also available in IP 67). They are color coded according to their voltage rating: yellow for 100/130V, blue for 200/250V, and red for 380/415V.

CEE 17 devices are available in a variety of ratings, including 16-amp, 32-amp, and 63-amp, but the 16-amp device is the most popular in our industry.

FIGURE 12.27
The CEE 17 16-amp connector is very popular in Europe and the UK for hard power or non-dimmed power.

IEC CONNECTORS

IEC 60320 is a standard that includes a range of plugs and receptacles, including the C13 receptacle and the C14 plug, colloquially known simply as IEC connectors. In North America, they are commonly used for desktop computers, lighting consoles, and other appliances. In Europe, they are sometimes used for hard power or non-dimmed loads, including luminaires.

FIGURE 12.28
IEC C13 receptacles and C14 plugs are commonly referred to simply as IEC connectors. They are used in North America to power lighting consoles, desktop computers, and appliances. In Europe they are used for a variety of applications, including powering some luminaires.

SCHUKO CONNECTORS

199

The CEE 7/4 or Type F connector is a two-pole three-wire connector with round pins and earthing clips on the side of the connector. It is commonly referred to as a Schuko connector. Schuko is short for *schukokontakt,* meaning "protective contact" in German. The name stems from the fact that a pair of earthing clips in the plug make contact with the protective earth in the recessed socket before the live and neutral pins are engaged.

FIGURE 12.29
A CEE 7/7 connector, commonly known as a Schuko connector, showing the two round pins and protective earth clip with a hole to mate with the male protective earth pin in the recessed socket.

Schuko connectors are commonly used on luminaires and dimmers in many parts of Europe. They are rated for 250 volts and up to 16 amps.

There are many more types of connectors in use throughout the world, but the connectors discussed here are a sampling of some of the more common ones used in North America and Europe.

UNDERSTANDING BEST PRACTICES, CODES, AND REGULATIONS

12.1   What is a company switch?

12.2   Why is it important not to make or break a feeder cable connection under load?

12.3   What is the most common type of cable used for portable single-conductor feeder cable or tails?

12.4   What is thermoset plastic (rubber)?

12.5   What is the difference between thermoset (rubber) and thermoplastic (PVC)?

12.6   What are some of the de-rating factors or correction factors that are taken into account when calculating the ampacity of wire and cable?

12.7   How many single-conductor connectors can be linked in a power distribution system?

12.8   What is the proper sequence for connecting feeder cable?

12.9   What protection is provided by a NEMA 3R connector?

12.10 What degree of protection is provided by an enclosure rated IP 65?

12.11 What is the NEMA enclosure rating that exceeds the requirements of IP 65?

12.12 Does a grounded conductor (neutral) count as a current-carrying conductor if the load is a balanced, three-phase conventional forward phase-control dimmer system? Why or why not?

12.13 In a power distribution system, what is meant by RGN? What is its purpose?

12.14 Why should a power distribution system remain on for 5 minutes after all of the discharge lamps have been dowsed at the end of a show?

12.15 Why are 37-pin circular connectors so rarely used in the entertainment production industry today?

12.16 If a 14-conductor cable is powering a series of portable dimmer packs and every circuit is connected to a load, how many current-carrying conductors are in the cable?

12.17   If a 14-conductor cable with a 90°C temperature rating is powering six 120V circuits, each with two 1200-watt single-channel dimmers, what size conductors (in AWG) should be used?

12.18   If we added a third single-channel dimmer pack to each circuit in the preceding question, and it also has a nameplate rating of 120V, 1200 watts, what size conductor and circuit breaker should be used?

12.19   What would happen to the pins and sockets in a stage pin connector if the pins became too compressed?

12.20   Is it permitted by code to use a NEMA 5-15P Edison plug to connect to a 20-amp receptacle?

12.21   What is the largest load in watts that a blue CEE 17 connector rated for 16 amps can handle in the UK?

12.22   What is the meaning of the German term *schukokontakt* and why is a connector named after it?

When I was in college studying electrical engineering, I worked in a petroleum refinery in Corpus Christi, Texas every summer, first with the electrical department and later on with the engineering department. There was a bit of a rivalry between the two departments. Many of the electricians resented the electrical engineers because they earned much more money, and it often seemed to the blue collar electricians that the white collar engineers had no clue what was really going on in the field.

Having worked on both sides of the fence, I believe the truth is somewhere in the middle. An engineer freshly out of college with no experience has little idea of many real-world issues. It's one thing to design a system on paper, but it's quite another to construct it in the field and make it work safely and properly.

Corpus Christi is a hot, humid city on the Gulf Coast of south Texas. In the August heat, the plant could be a miserable place, with rancid smells and hot wind blowing through the dusty caliche roads. The field workers — the electricians, pipe fitters, welders, and mechanics — tried their level best to get as much work done as possible in the relative cool of the early morning and spend as much time as possible in the shop during the heat of the day.

There was one older electrician named Walter who had been working at the plant for over 40 years. He lived outside of Corpus Christi in the town of Victoria, which is about an hour-and-a-half drive to and from work each day. He used to get up at 4:30 a.m., get dressed, have breakfast, and leave the house by 5:15 so he could be at work by 6:45, well before the 7:00 a.m. whistle blew.

One particularly hot summer we were working a turnaround, which is when a section of the refinery is shut down to rework it or to do main-

tenance and repair. It costs the refinery a lot of money for any part of the plant to be idle, so during turnarounds, we would work 12-hour days, seven days a week. The engineers used to come out periodically to monitor the work and check on the progress, but for the most part, they would stay in their air-conditioned offices during the hottest part of the day. When they did show up in the field, the electricians liked to give them a hard time, albeit in a jesting manner.

One day, a young engineer by the name of Arturo came by at the end of the day to check up on the work being done. The electrical crew was busy making terminations on a very large panel with hundreds of terminals. Arturo made a cutting remark about the slow progress within the earshot of half of the crew. Their ears perked.

"Well, if you're so smart," said one of the electricians, "why don't you pick up a screwdriver and we'll see what you can do."

"I can make these terminations at least as fast as you guys," Art said. The gauntlet had been thrown down.

They set up a contest between the fastest electrician and the engineer. They would see who could make the most terminations in five minutes. Since it was late in the day, they planned to stage a race first thing in the morning.

The next day, the entire engineering staff showed up to watch the event. The electrical crew was ready. But instead of the young Arturo working at the panel, the engineers substituted Bill, a much more experienced engineer.

At the signal, two men started working. Much to the delight of the electrical crew, the engineer struggled. He had a hard time loosening the terminals and a hard time tightening them down. There was no contest. The electrician won by a Texas mile. The engineers cried foul, made excuses, and left with their tails tucked between their legs.

The next day, Walter told me that he had fixed the contest. He had taken his wife's fingernail polish and dabbed it under each of the terminals on the engineer's panel so that they would be harder to loosen. Then he ground down the tip of the screwdriver that was given to the engineer to use just enough so that it wasn't noticeable but enough to slow him down.

I learned a couple of lessons that summer, the kind of lesson that you can't learn from books or from your college professor. There was the lesson about respecting the people you work with — it's never a good idea to taunt them — and then there's the lesson about the difference between engineering know how and field experience. But the most important lesson I learned that summer was this: when you have something to prove, *never* be the *second* one to show up to work.

Part of not being second to show up for work is a metaphor for striving to be the best. If you are well prepared, have knowledge of your profession and experience in the field, and treat everyone you encounter with the respect they deserve, you will *be* the best. Whether it's punching the clock, logging time on the job, or logging time reading and preparing, always strive to do your best and you will be richly rewarded. And always remember this: safety comes first.

Appendix 1
Useful Formulas

Ohm's law: V (volts) = I (amps) × R (ohms)

Single-phase AC power = V (volts) × I (amps) × Power factor

Three-phase AC power = V (volts) × I (amps) × Power factor × 1.732

Power factor = cosine (phase angle) × 100
= Power (watts) ÷ [V (volts) × I (amps)]

Apparent power (watts) = V (volts) × I (amps)

$V_{peak} = V_{rms} \times 1.414$

$V_{rms} = V_{peak} \times 0.7071$

Inductive reactance = X_L (ohms) = $2\pi f L$, where X_L is the inductive reactance, π is pi (3.14), f is the frequency in hertz, and L is the inductance in henrys

Capacitive reactance = $X_C = \dfrac{1}{2\pi f C}$, where X_C is the capacitive

reactance, f is the frequency, and C is the capacitance in farads

Series resistance: $R_{total} = R_1 + R_2 + \ldots + R_{n-1} + R_n$, where $n =$ the total number of resistors in series

Parallel resistance: $\dfrac{1}{R_{total}} = \dfrac{1}{R_1} + \dfrac{1}{R_2} + \cdots + \dfrac{1}{R_{n-1}} + \dfrac{1}{R_n}$, where

R_{total} is the total resistance, R_1 is the first resistor, R_2 is the second resistor, R_{n-1} is the second to last resistor, and R_n is the last resistor.

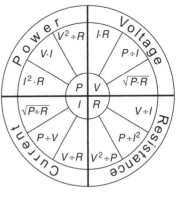

1 inch = 0.0254 meters = 2.54 centimeters = 25.4 millimeters

1 centimeter = 0.3937 inches = 10 millimeters = 0.01 meters

1 millimeter = 0.1 centimeters = 0.001 meters = 0.03937 inches

1 kilometer = 3280.84 feet = 0.62137 miles = 1093.67 yards

1 meter = 1000 millimeters = 100 centimeters = 39.37 inches
= 3.28084 feet = 1.09361 yards

1 mile = 1609.34 meters = 1.60934 kilometers = 5280 feet
= 1760 yards

1 yard = 914.4 millimeters = 91.44 centimeters = 36 inches
= 0.9144 meters = 3 feet

Temperature in °C = (temperature in °F − 32) ÷ 1.8

Temperature in °F = (temperature in °C × 1.8) + 32

Horsepower = Watts ÷ 746 × Efficiency

	joules	watt-hours	kilowatt-hours	megawatt-hours	BTUs
1 joule	= 1 joule	= 2.78×10^{-4} watt-hours	= 2.78×10^{-7} kilowatt-hours	= 2.78×10^{-10} megawatt-hours	= 9.478×10^{-4} BTUs
1 watt-hour	= 3600 joules	= 1 watt-hour	= 0.001 kilowatt-hours	= 10^{-6} megawatt-hours	= 3.413 BTUs
1 kilowatt-hour	= 3.6×10^{6} joules	= 1000 watt-hours	= 1 kilowatt-hour	= 0.001 megawatt-hours	= 3413 BTUs
1 megawatt-hour	= 3.6×10^{9} joules	= 10^{6} watt-hours	= 1000 kilowatt-hours	= 1 megawatt-hour	= 3.413×10^{6} BTUs
1 BTU	= 1055.06 joules	= 0.293 watt-hours	= 2.93×10^{-4} kilowatt-hours	= 2.93×10^{-7} megawatt-hours	= 1 BTU

Appendix 4
Scientific, Exponential, and Engineering Notation

SI Prefix	Scientific Notation	Exponential Notation	Engineering Notation	Decimal Equivalent
Pico	10^{-12}	E-12	10^{-12}	0.000 000 000 001
Nano	10^{-9}	E-9	10^{-9}	0.000 000 001
Micro	10^{-6}	E-6	10^{-6}	0.000 001
Milli	10^{-3}	E-3	10^{-3}	0.001
Centi	10^{-2}	E-2	n/a	0.01
Deci	10^{-1}	E-1	n/a	0.1
—	10^{0}	E+0	n/a	1
Deca	10^{1}	E+1	n/a	10
Hecto	10^{2}	E+2	n/a	100
Kilo	10^{3}	E+3	10^{3}	1000
Mega	10^{6}	E+6	10^{6}	1,000,000
Giga	10^{9}	E+9	10^{9}	1,000,000,000
Tera	10^{12}	E+12	10^{12}	1,000,000,000,000

CHAPTER 1   ANSWERS

1.1   Electricity is the transfer of energy through the motion of charge-carrying electrons.

1.2   False; subatomic particles are smaller than atoms.

1.3 10^{-12} meters in diameter

1.4   Electrons, protons, and neutrons

1.5   13

1.6   Half

1.7   Coulomb's law

1.8   Ionized

1.9   The coulomb

1.10 6.241506×10^{18}

1.11   (a) Positive; (b) 1/4X coulombs

1.12   (a) 4Y newtons; (b) 16Y newtons

1.13   An atom that is missing an electron from its outer orbit or shell

1.14   Near the speed of light

1.15   Because the electrons in the outer orbit of an insulator are very tightly bound to the nucleus and they are not easily freed

1.16   Tungsten

1.17   Conductivity

1.18   Because current convention was established before the knowledge that it was produced by the flow of negative charges

1.19   Conventional current flow is away from the positive terminal of a battery because the positive terminal attracts negative charge, which is the opposite of conventional current flow.

CHAPTER 2   ANSWERS

2.1   Voltage

2.2   Both are examples of potential energy.

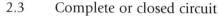

2.3   Complete or closed circuit

2.4   Opposition

2.5   Rate at which work is being done

2.6   Yes

2.7   Yes

2.8   True

2.9   Time

2.10   Created; destroyed

2.11   No

2.12   The meter, the kilogram, the second, the amp, the kelvin, the mole, and the candela

2.13   Current

2.14   The potential difference across a 1-watt load with a current of 1 amp

2.15   The amount of resistance that will produce a voltage drop of 1 volt given a current of 1 amp

2.16   Conductance

2.17   0.278 watt-hours

2.18   3413 BTUs

CHAPTER 3   ANSWERS

3.1   3.84 ohms

3.2   More than 4 ohms

3.3   1500 volts

3.4   90 volts

3.5   0.16 amps

3.6   1.8 ohms

3.7   200 ohms

3.8   12 amps

3.9   24 ohms

3.10   100 millivolts

3.11   120 watts

3.12   12.5 amps

3.13   10.42 amps

3.14   2.4 ohms

3.15   56.25 watts

3.16 2.35×10^6

3.17   0.00000566

3.18 8.125×10^6 watts

CHAPTER 4   ANSWERS

4.1   (a) They provided the means to build an AC induction motor, which, until Tesla's work, was unavailable and thus AC was not as useful as DC. (b) They provided the means for creating a centralized AC power generation model as opposed to a distributed DC model.

4.2   The magnetic dipole

4.3   Because they are randomly aligned in most materials and the magnetic fields cancel

4.4   True

4.5   True

4.6   Lines of flux

4.7   Changing

4.8   The voltage in a loop of wire is proportional to the rate of change of a magnetic field through the wire.

4.9   Parallel, perpendicular

4.10 $\sin 30° = x/(3\,\text{cm/second}); x = 3 \times \sin 30° = 3 \times 0.5 = 1.5\,\text{cm/second}$

4.11   True

4.12   False; it indicates the direction of the force applied to a conductor moving through a magnetic field in a generator.

4.13 $-0.643; -1$

4.14   Because they are both the same point on the circle

4.15 $V_{instantaneous} = V_{peak} \times \sin \theta = 169.7 \times \sin 20° = 58.04$ volts

4.16   34.2 volts

4.17   Speed of rotation (RPM) × number of poles
       = 120 × frequency (Hz)

$$\text{Speed of rotation} = (120 \times 60) \div 16 = 450\,\text{RPM}$$

4.18   0.02 seconds

4.19   Speed of rotation (RPM) × number of poles
       = 120 × frequency (Hz)

$$\text{Speed of rotation} = (120 \times 50) \div 8 = 750\,\text{RPM}$$

217

4.20   0.984808

4.21   50 Hz; 60 Hz

4.22   See graphic on page 57.

4.23   325.3 volts

4.24   Because more sample points yield a more accurate answer. We would have to sample an infinite number of points to get the final answer.

4.25   No, because the RMS value and the average value (with the negative half cycle inverted) are not the same. The RMS value is the equivalent of the power transfer from a DC source.

CHAPTER 5   ANSWERS

5.1   (a) 198 159.5 ohms; (b) 55 000 ohms; (c) 54 782 ohms; (d) 53 571 ohms

5.2   By replacing the series resistors within the parallel resistor networks, we can replace the entire resistor network with the following:

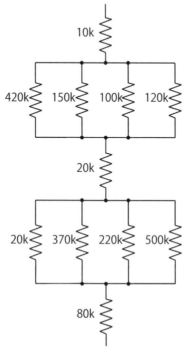

FIGURE A5.1

The next step is to replace the two parallel networks within the entire resistor network as follows:

Finally, the five series resistors can be added to find the result.

$$R_{total} = 10k + 36.5k + 20k + 16.88k + 80k = 163.38k \text{ ohms}$$

5.3

$$V = I \times R$$

$$6.6 \text{ volts} = I \times (0.011 \times 20)$$

$$I = 6.6 \div 0.22 = 30 \text{ amps}$$

5.4 First, calculate the total allowable resistance, and then find the length of cable that would produce that resistance.

$$V = I \times R$$

$$9.2 = 16 \times R$$

$$R = 9.2 \div 16 = 0.575 \text{ ohms}$$

$$\text{Length} = R \div \text{characteristic resistance (ohms/meter)}$$
$$= 0.575 \div 0.029 = 19.83 \text{ meters}$$

5.5

$$V = I \times R$$

$$V = 45 \times (0.0073 \times 40) = 13.14 \text{ volts}$$

5.6 There are 3.28 feet per meter, or 3280 feet per 1000 meters. So we can calculate the resistance of 1 foot of the wire. 5.20864 ohms per 1000 meters = 5.20864 ohms per 3280 feet, or 0.001588 ohms per foot.

If the entire circuit has 500 feet of wire (250 feet to the load and 250 feet back to the PD), then we can calculate the total resistance as follows:

$$R_{total} = 0.001588 \text{ ohms per foot} \times 500 \text{ feet} = 0.79 \text{ ohms}$$

5.7 We can use Ohm's law to calculate the voltage drop of this circuit using the resistance that we calculated above (0.79 ohms)

10k

36.5k

20k

16.88k

80k

FIGURE A5.2

219

and the maximum current before tripping the circuit breaker (20 amps).

$$V = I \times R$$

In this case, I = 20 amps and R = 0.79 ohms. Therefore,

$$V = 20\, \text{amps} \times 0.79\, \text{ohms} = 15.9\, \text{volts}$$

If our calculations are correct, then 500 feet of #12 AWG wire carrying 20 amps will produce a 15.9-volt drop across the entire run of wire. The circuit consisting of a 250-foot run of wire connected to the load and another 250-foot run of wire back to the panel can be represented by three resistors in series across the supply voltage. The first resistor is the equivalent resistance of a 250-foot run of wire, the second is the resistance of the load, and the third is another 250-foot run of wire.

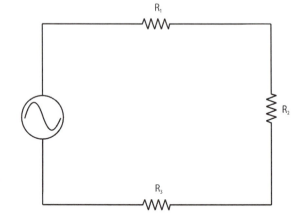

FIGURE A5.3
A load connected across two long runs of wire is like a circuit with three resistors connected in series where the first is the resistance of the wire, the second is the load, and the third is the return wire.

5.8   We can calculate the resistance of the lamp filament at the given voltage using the following power formula:

$$R = V^2 \div W$$

$$R = 120^2 \div 1000$$

$$R = 14400 \div 1000$$

$$R = 14.4\, \text{ohms}$$

Using the value of the resistance for #12 AWG we calculated in the example above (0.001588 ohms per foot), we can draw the equivalent circuit as shown in the figure below:

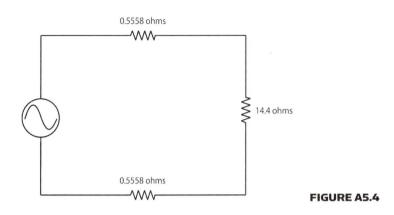

0.5558 ohms

14.4 ohms

0.5558 ohms

FIGURE A5.4

5.9   By combining the circuit resistance, we can calculate the current in the circuit as shown below:

$$I = V \div R$$

$$I = 120 \text{ volts} \div (0.5558 + 14.4 + 0.5558) \text{ ohms}$$

$$I = 120 \div 15.51$$

$$I = 7.736 \text{ amps}$$

Now that we know the current flowing through the circuit, we can calculate the voltage drop across each circuit element using the following voltage formula:

$$V = I \times R$$

$$V_1 = 7.736 \times 0.5558 = 4.3 \text{ volts}$$

$$V_2 = 7.74 \times 14.4 = 111.4 \text{ volts}$$

$$V_3 = 7.74 \times 0.5558 = 4.3 \text{ volts}$$

V_2 is the voltage across the lamp, which is 111.5 volts. We can confirm our work by adding the voltages across each circuit element, which should add up to the applied voltage.

221

$$V_{total} = V_1 + V_2 + V_3$$

$$V_{total} = 4.3 + 111.4 + 4.3 = 12 \text{ volts}$$

5.10 Four percent of 230 volts is 9.2 volts (230×0.04), so we need to find the length of cable that will produce that voltage drop at 15 amps and ensure that we don't exceed it. We can use Ohm's law to calculate the allowable resistance for the entire length of the run, and then use the characteristic resistance of the wire to find out what that length is.

$$V = I \times R$$

$$9.2 \text{ volts} = 15 \text{ amps} \times R$$

$$R = 9.2 \div 15 = 0.613 \text{ ohms}$$

If the characteristic resistance of the wire is 0.029 ohms per meter, then the length of wire with a total resistance of 0.613 ohms is:

$$\text{Distance (meters)} = 0.613 \text{ ohms} \div 0.029 \text{ ohms per meter}$$

$$\text{Distance} = 21.15 \text{ meters}$$

5.11 Resistance; reactance

5.12 Inductance

5.13 Electric charge

5.14 The magnetic field set up by the flow of current resists the changing direction of AC current and the reversing magnetic field.

5.15

$$X_L = 2\pi fL$$

$$X_L = 2 \times \pi \times 60 \times 0.250$$

$$X_L = 94.25 \text{ ohms}$$

5.16 First, we need to calculate the inductive reactance:

$$X_L = 2\pi fL$$

$$X_L = 2 \times \pi \times 60 \times 0.750$$

$$X_L = 282.74 \text{ ohms}$$

Next, we can calculate the current:

$$V = I \times X_L$$

$$120 \text{ volts} = I \times 282.74$$

$$I = 120 \div 282.74 = 0.42 \text{A}$$

5.17 Open circuit

5.18

$$X_C = \frac{1}{2\pi fC}$$

$$X_C = \frac{1}{2 \times \pi \times 50 \times 0.00075}$$

$$X_C = \frac{1}{.2356}$$

$$X_C = 4.24 \text{ ohms}$$

5.19 Voltage; current

5.20 Magnitude; direction

5.21 First, calculate the inductive reactance and the capacitive reactance:

$$X_L = 2\pi fL$$

$$X_L = 2 \times \pi \times 60 \times 0.15$$

$$X_L = 56.55 \text{ ohms}$$

$$X_C = \frac{1}{2\pi fC}$$

$$X_C = \frac{1}{2 \times \pi \times 60 \times 0.00025}$$

$$X_C = \frac{1}{.0942}$$

$$X_C = 10.61 \text{ ohms}$$

Next, we calculate the impedance:

$$Z^2 = R^2 + (X_L - X_C)^2$$

$$Z^2 = 150^2 + (56.55 - 10.61)^2$$

$$Z^2 = 22.5 \times 10^3 + (45.94)^2$$

$$Z^2 = 22.5 \times 10^3 + 2110.5$$

$$Z = \sqrt{24610.5}$$

$$Z = 156.88 \text{ ohms}$$

5.22　First, we sum the vectors of the inductive reactance and the capacitive reactance as shown in the figure below.

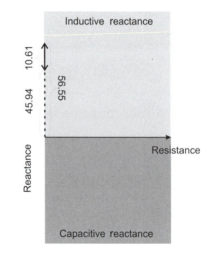

FIGURE A5.5

Reactance = 56.55 − 10.61 ohms = 45.94 ohms

Since the magnitude of the inductive reactance is larger than the magnitude of the capacitive reactance, the sum is more inductive.

Next, we vectorially sum the inductive reactance and the resistance as shown in the following figure:

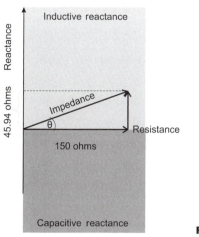

FIGURE A5.6

Now we can use the formula for tangents to calculate the phase angle.

$$\tan\theta = \text{opposite side} \div \text{adjacent side} = 45.94 \div 150$$

$$\theta = \arctan(0.306)$$

$$\theta = 17°$$

5.23

$$V_{\text{out}} = V_{\text{in}} \times \frac{\text{turns (secondary)}}{\text{turns (primary)}}$$

$$240 = 480 \times \frac{\text{turns (secondary)}}{200}$$

$$\text{turns (secondary)} = (240 \times 200) \div 480 = 100 \text{ turns}$$

5.24

$$V_{\text{sec}} = V_{\text{pri}} \times \frac{\text{turns-secondary}}{\text{turns-primary}}$$

$$13{,}000 = V_{\text{pri}} \times \frac{130}{10}$$

$$V_{\text{pri}} = 13{,}000 \times 10 \div 130 = 1000 \text{ volts}$$

5.25   Step up

CHAPTER 6   ANSWERS

6.1   cos 30° = 0.866; therefore, the real power = 86.6% of maximum

6.2   (a) Because the cosine of 90° is 0; (b) because the product of two sinewaves that are 90° out of phase with each other is a third sinewave of twice the frequency, half of which is positive and half of which is negative, and the two halves cancel each other out

6.3   It implies that the load is sending power back to the supply.

6.4   When the DC voltage and current match the AC RMS voltage and current, and the phase angle is 0°

6.5   24.15°

6.6   0.64

6.7   No, because the cosine of an angle can never be greater than 1.

6.8   Because it requires more current-handling capability, including bigger transformers, switches, cables, transmission towers, labor, and other resources, for the same amount of power transferred

6.9   Because there is less current flowing through it, it can use smaller wires, fuses, components, and hardware.

6.10   If it's an inductive load, add a power factor correction capacitor; if it's a capacitive load, add a power factor correction inductor.

6.11   It moves back and forth between the load and the source.

6.12   Power that does no work, i.e., reactive power

6.13   Power that does work; the power consumed by a load

6.14   The vector sum of real and reactive power

6.15   1560 watts

6.16

$$\text{Phase angle} = \text{inverse}\,(\cos 0.93) = 21.6°$$

$$\text{Real power}\,(\text{watts}) = 220\,\text{volts} \times 8.3\,\text{amps} \times 0.93$$

$$\text{Real power}\,(\text{watts}) = 1698.2\,\text{watts}$$

$$\text{Reactive power} = \sqrt{(\text{Apparent power}^2 - \text{Real power}^2)}$$

$$\text{Reactive power} = \sqrt{(1826^2 - 1698.2^2)} = 671.1\,\text{watts}$$

6.17   Referring to Figure A5.7 below, we can see the relationship between the apparent power, real power, and reactive power. We are given the apparent power (15,000 watts) and the reactive power (2500 watts), so we can use the following equation to solve for the real power.

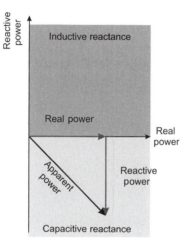

FIGURE A5.7

$$|\text{Apparent power}| = \sqrt{(\text{Real power}^2 + \text{Reactive power}^2)}$$

$$15{,}000 = \sqrt{(\text{Real power}^2 + 2500^2)}$$

$$\text{Real power} = \sqrt{(15000^2 - 2500^2)} = 14{,}790.2 \text{ watts}$$

Now that we know the magnitude of the three sides of the right power triangle, we can solve for the phase angle.

$$\cos(\text{phase angle}) = \text{Real power} \div \text{Apparent power}$$

$$\cos(\text{phase angle}) = 14{,}790.2 \div 15{,}000 = 0.986$$

$$\text{Phase angle} = \text{inverse}[\cos(0.986)] = 9.6°$$

6.18

$$\text{Three-phase balanced AC power (watts)}$$
$$= \text{Voltage (volts)} \times \text{Current (amps)} \times$$
$$\text{Power factor} \times 1.73$$

$$\text{Power} = 208\text{V} \times 5\text{A} \times 0.9 \times 1.732 = 1621.2 \text{ watts}$$

6.19

$$\text{Power} = (\text{Horsepower} \times 746) \div \text{Efficiency}$$

$$\text{Power} = (41.7 \times 746) \div 0.94 = 33,093.8 \text{ watts}$$

6.20

$$\text{Three-phase balanced AC power (watts)}$$
$$= \text{Voltage (volts)} \times \text{Current (amps)} \times$$
$$\text{Power factor} \times 1.73$$

$$33,093.8 \text{ watts} = 460 \times \text{Current} \times 0.80 \times 1.73$$

$$\text{Current} = 33,093.8 \div (460 \times 0.80 \times 1.73) = 51.98 \text{ amps}$$

CHAPTER 7   ANSWERS

7.1   Voltage, current, waveform, AC or DC, frequency, length of time of exposure, body shape, age, weight, sex, the path of current, amount of clothing, amount of moisture

7.2   About 1000 ohms

7.3   The fluttering or twitching of the heart; the rapid irregular contractions of the heart

7.4   100 to 300 milliamps (0.1 to 0.3 amps)

7.5   Wear gloves, rubber-soled shoes, long cotton pants and shirt, a hat, and thick socks; take off dangling jewelry; stand on carpet; don't stand in water

7.6   Because synthetic fiber will melt to the skin and aggravate a burn

7.7   The heart, lungs, and brain

7.8   About 500 ohms

7.9   The minimum amount of current that a person can perceive; it's about 0.2 to 0.5 milliamps for most people

7.10   About 0.5 milliamps

7.11   Because if you're walking a truss or standing on a ladder you could fall off.

7.12   30 milliamps

7.13   In the event that it is not dead, they won't be frozen to the circuit by being unable to let go.

7.14   10 milliamps to 60 milliamps

7.15   Arc flash burns

7.16   It's when the air around a conductor becomes ionized and changes from an insulator to a conductor, and then the conductor discharges and creates an extremely hot plasma ball.

7.17   It can be as high as 19,427°C (35,000° F).

7.18   It is an explosive blast with very high pressure created by an arc flash.

7.19   It vaporizes and expands up to 67,000 times.

7.20   Ruptured eardrums, collapsed lungs, concussions, internal organ damage

7.21   Dust, impurities, corrosion, moisture, human contact, dropped tools, high voltage, insulation breakdown

7.22   It's the boundary within which a person could receive a second-degree burn in the event of an arc flash.

7.23   4 feet

7.24   It's a procedure to ensure that a circuit is de-energized, locked out, and tested before any work is done on it.

7.25   So that it won't be unknowingly unlocked in the event of a miscommunication

CHAPTER 8   ANSWERS

8.1   (1) There must be a voltage difference between two points in the circuit, and (2) there must be a complete path of conductive material between the two points.

8.2   Complete circuit

8.3   It serves to stabilize the voltage in the event of a lightning strike or voltage surge and to provide a common reference.

8.4   In the event that a live conductor comes in contact with a conductive part, the grounding conductor will cause a large current to flow to ground and trip the overcurrent protective device.

8.5   Reference point

8.6   The equipment enclosure will become energized, and anyone who touches it will complete the path to ground, causing current to flow through them.

8.7   They are bonded to the system grounding conductor or circuit protective conductor.

8.8   Earth

8.9   The neutral conductor

8.10   The grounded conductor is the neutral and the grounding conductor is the equipment ground.

8.11   Bonding is the mechanical and electrical connection between metal parts and enclosures and the system grounding conductor. Grounding is the low-impedance path to the grounding rod or earthing rod.

8.12   Service entrance

8.13   A uni-grounded system has only one grounding or earthing rod, while a multi-grounded system is grounded at the utility pole and at the electrical outlet.

8.14   The potential hazard is that there could be a large difference in voltage between the grounded conductor and any of the system grounds, creating a potential for electric shock. This problem is typically addressed by the use of residual current devices (RCDs).

8.15   Because there could be a high potential between the system ground and the signal ground or equipment chassis. Anyone who touches the equipment chassis or signal ground and another grounded point at the same time can receive a lethal shock.

CHAPTER 9   ANSWERS

9.1   It's an inverse-time relationship, meaning that the fuse will blow faster with a higher current.

9.2   Because they could short circuit by arcing across the terminals if the applied voltage exceeds the rated voltage

9.3   You shouldn't replace an IEC fuse with a UL or CSA fuse, and vice versa, because the methods of rating fuses are different.

9.4   You should use a fuse rated for at least 22.86 amps (70% of 22.86 is 16 amps).

9.5   30; 1000

9.6   To allow for high inrush currents normally associated with discharge lamps, motors, transformers, and other capacitive or inductive loads

9.7   To quench the arc in the event of a blown fuse and to absorb the heat generated by the arc

9.8   Current flows through a bi-metallic strip made of two metals with dissimilar coefficients of expansion. When the current is high enough, the metal strip bends and trips a spring-loaded mechanism that opens the contacts and shuts off the current.

9.9   Because it takes time for the bi-metallic strip to heat up and trip the breaker

9.10   The thermal mechanism provides protection against overloading the circuit while the magnetic sensor provides faster-acting short circuit protection.

9.11   The current flowing through a magnetic circuit breaker produces a magnetic field in a solenoid, which moves an iron core in proportion to the strength of the current. When the current reaches a predetermined level, the iron core triggers the circuit breaker.

9.12   Magnetic

9.13   The ambient temperature affects the starting temperature of the bi-metallic strip in thermal circuit breakers. In high ambient temperatures the tripping current is reduced, and in low ambient temperatures it is increased. The ambient temperature does not affect magnetic circuit breakers.

9.14   A terra-terra (T-T) system of power distribution is earthed at the utility pole and at the point where power is being consumed.

9.15   An RCD, or residual current device, is a circuit breaker designed to trip if there is a difference of at least 30 milliamps between the outgoing current and the return current.

9.16 A GFCI, or ground fault circuit interrupter, is a circuit breaker designed to trip if there is a difference of at least 6 milliamps between the outgoing current and the return current.

9.17 The difference between an RCD and a GFCI is that an RCD uses an electromechanical relay to open the breaker contacts at a level of 30 milliamps and a GFCI uses an electronic circuit to open the breaker contacts at a level of 6 milliamps. GFCIs are more accurate than RCDs.

9.18 A Class A GFCI is designed to protect personnel by tripping at 6 milliamps. Class B GFCIs are obsolete; they were designed to trip at 20 milliamps.

9.19 No, it covers electrical services of 100 amps or less, 120–240VAC single- and three-phase 60-Hz circuits where the voltage to ground does not exceed 150VAC.

9.20 GFCIs should be used in any outdoor, wet, or damp locations.

9.21 Yes.

9.22 GFCIs should not be used for branch circuits power egress lighting, for exit lighting, for emergency lighting systems, or if tripping the GFCI could cause injury.

9.23 Standard GFCIs are disallowed for use in dimmed circuits because the electronic components in the GFCI need constant power to operate correctly and because the third-order harmonics generated by conventional forward-phase dimmers can be interpreted by GFCIs as current leakage, which can cause nuisance tripping.

9.24 Yes, but it's not recommended.

9.25 Voltage surges, lighting strikes.

CHAPTER 10   ANSWERS

10.1 The common node connects to the neutral conductor and the system grounding conductor.

10.2 You can get 208 volts by connecting from phase to phase and 120 volts by connecting from phase to neutral.

10.3 The allowable voltage range is 230V + 10%/−6%, or 216.2 volts to 253 volts.

10.4 $V_{p-p} = V_{p-n} \times 1.732 = 398.26V$

10.5   The angles of any triangle always add up to 180°. We know that the angle AOB is 120° because in a three-phase system, the two phases are 120° apart. Therefore, the sum of angles OAB and OBA must be 60°. We also know by looking at Figure 10.4 on page 136 that the angles OAB and OBA are equal. Therefore, we can conclude that the angle OAB is 30°. Since the angle of vector OA is 0°, the angle of the vector AO is 180°. If the vector AB is 30° ahead of AO, then by deduction we know that the vector AB is 150°.

10.6   See above.

10.7   The split-phase voltage (or the phase-to-neutral voltage) is 100 volts at 50 Hz.

10.8   The phase-to-phase voltage in a three-phase delta system is twice the phase-to-neutral voltage because the two halves of the phase-to-phase voltage are in phase with each other.

10.9   A single-phase, three-wire plus ground system uses a split-phase distribution transformer to tap into a three-phase delta transmission system to supply power to individual consumers.

10.10   A single-phase three-wire plus ground earthed midpoint system has a center-tapped transformer that allows the consumer to have the full phase voltage or half of the phase voltage. A single-phase three-wire plus ground earthed end-of-phase system has no center tap and it supplies only one voltage, which is the full phase to ground voltage.

10.11   No, they vary from country to country.

10.12   There are no phase colors designated by the NEC, but the de facto standard is black for phase A, red for phase B, and blue for phase C.

10.13   In Europe, the circuit protective conductor is green with a yellow stripe and the neutral is blue.

10.14   No current flows in the neutral as long as the load is balanced between the three phases because they cancel in the neutral conductor.

10.15   No current flows in the neutral as long as the load is balanced between the two phase conductors because they cancel in the neutral conductor.

CHAPTER 11   ANSWERS

11.1   50%

11.2   Because an SCR is a directional device and it can only conduct current in one direction; therefore, it doesn't work during half of the voltage cycle. A triac is a bidirectional device and it can conduct in either direction.

11.3   Filament sing is caused by the mechanical vibration of the filament, which is produced by the current overshooting its steady-state operating level.

11.4   To reduce filament sing in a forward-phase dimmer, a choke is inserted in the current path to restrict the sudden rise in current.

11.5   The rise time is the time, measured in microseconds, it takes for the current to reach its correct level after a dimmer switches on during the voltage cycle.

11.6   A reverse phase-control dimmer is one that switches the voltage off during the voltage cycle as opposed to switching it on, as in a conventional forward phase-control dimmer. It uses an IGBT or similar switching transistor that can handle large currents and turn on or off at any time during the voltage cycle. It uses this type of switching device because a triac or SCR can only turn on during the voltage cycle but can't turn off until the voltage is at zero.

11.7   It should turn on at 180° and back off again at 215° so the two half cycles will be symmetrical, thus avoiding creating a DC offset.

11.8   Reverse phase-control dimmers are lighter than forward phase-control dimmers because they don't need a choke to limit the rise time, and they are more expensive because high-current switching transistors like IGBTs are more expensive than triacs or SCRs.

11.9   The fundamental frequency is 120 Hz; the second harmonic frequency is 240 Hz; the third harmonic frequency is 360 Hz.

11.10   Because they can be used to construct any other waveform by adding sinewaves that are whole number multiples of the fundamental frequency with various amplitudes

11.11 See instructions.

11.12 The triplens sum in the neutral because the third-order harmonics produced by the three phase conductors are in phase and reinforce each other, while the fundamentals and the second-order harmonics are out of phase and cancel in the neutral conductor.

11.13 The dimming level would be 25%.

11.14 A linear load is one that draws current from the source in a linear fashion; if the voltage input is a sinewave, then the output is a sinewave. A conventional forward phase-control dimmer is not a linear load because the output is not the same waveform as the input voltage. A sinewave dimmer is a linear load.

11.15 A K-rated transformer has bigger conductors, special winding geometry, heat-managing cooling ducts, bigger iron cores, and an oversized neutral terminal to better handle the heat generated by third-order harmonics.

11.16 The K factor, or factor K, is a measure of the amount of heat generated in a transformer due to the harmonic content based on the ratio of the harmonic content of a waveform compared to the overall current.

11.17 According to an article written by Steve Terry in the Summer 2002 issue of *Protocol Magazine* (published by ESTA, www.esta .org) called "Power Play: Considerations for Feeding Permanent Dimmer-per-Circuit Systems," the K rating for a typical conventional forward phase-control dimmer system should be K-13.

11.18 The windings in an HMT are arranged so that the magnetic flux due to the harmonic currents in the three phases of a three-phase system cancel each other, thus preventing the harmonic currents from circulating.

11.19 Another name for an HMT is a zigzag transformer.

11.20 A harmonic suppression system blocks triplens with the use of a tuned RLC circuit, preventing them from circulating in the system.

CHAPTER 12   ANSWERS

12.1 A company switch is an enclosure with a disconnect and single-pole connector taps that allows a visiting company to safely tie in their feeder cable and power distribution system.

235

12.2   It's important not to make or break feeder cable connections under load because it is extremely dangerous. Breaking a connection under load will draw an arc, which could jump to the person holding the connector, and making a connection under load could cause an arc flash.

12.3   The most common type of cable used for portable single-conductor feeder cable or tails is type SC, which is jacketed with a thermoset (or rubber) outer covering.

12.4   Thermoset is a type of plastic that cures or hardens through the application of heat and forms a more durable compound.

12.5   Thermoset (rubber) hardens only once through the application of heat, while thermoplastic (PVC) retains its plasticity through multiple heating and cooling cycles.

12.6   Some of the de-rating factors or correction factors that are taken into account when calculating the ampacity of wire and cable are ambient temperature, the temperature rating of the insulation, voltage drop, and the number of cables that are grouped together.

12.7   Up to three connector pairs can be linked together in the first 100 feet (30 meters), and one connector pair can be used for each additional 100 feet (30 meters).

12.8   The correct sequence for connecting single-conductor feeder cable is grounding conductor or protective ground first, grounded conductor or neutral second, and phase conductors last.

12.9   NEMA 3R connectors provide a degree of protection to personnel against incidental contact with the live components and against falling dirt, rain, sleet, and snow, and they are undamaged by the external formation of ice. They can be used indoors or outdoors.

12.10 An enclosure rated IP 65 is dust tight and protects against low-pressure water jetting from all sides.

12.11 A NEMA 4 or NEMA 4X enclosure exceeds the requirements for IP 65.

12.12 Yes, a grounded conductor (neutral conductor) does count as a current-carrying conductor in a balanced, three-phase dimming system because a conventional forward phase-control dimming system produces third-order harmonics (or triplens) that cause current to flow in the neutral.

12.13   In a power distribution system, RGN stands for reversed neutral and ground. It is a practice that is sometimes used to prevent the accidental connection of the grounded conductor or grounding conductor to the phase conductors.

12.14   The power distribution system should remain on for 5 minutes after all of the discharge lamps have been dowsed at the end of a show so that the internal fans in the luminaires can cool the lamps properly.

12.15   Because 12-circuit multiconductor cables are big, heavy, and expensive. Also, these connectors were used for 0–10V lighting control, which has become virtually obsolete since multiplexed lighting control (DMX512) was introduced.

12.16   If a 14-conductor cable is powering a series of portable dimmer packs and every circuit is connected to a load, then there are 12 current-carrying conductors.

12.17   If a 14-conductor cable with a temperature rating of 90°C is connected to two 120V, 1200-watt dimmers per circuit, then there are 12 current-carrying conductors in the cable. According to Table 12.6 on page 191, a cable with 12 current-carrying conductors should be de-rated to 70% of its maximum ampacity. Therefore, we need to find the current in each of the six circuits and size the conductors based on a 70% de-rating factor. A 120V circuit with two 1200-watt dimmers will draw 20 amps (assuming a power factor of 1). Checking Table 12.5 on page 191, we can see that a #14 AWG conductor with a 90°C insulation will carry 28 amps. But if we take into account the 70% de-rating factor, then it is only allowed to carry a maximum of 19.6 amps, which is not enough for our load. Therefore, we have to go up to a #12 AWG conductor, which carries 24.5 amps with a 70% de-rating factor and 90°C temperature rating. Since that is enough to carry the required 20 amps per circuit and the maximum rating of the circuit breaker is 20 amps, the 19-conductor cable can have #12 AWG conductors.

12.18   If we add another single-channel, 120V, 1200-watt dimmer to each of the six circuits in our 19-conductor cable, then that would add another 10 amps per circuit for a total of 30 amps. With a de-rating factor of 70%, we would need a conductor with an ampacity rating of at least 42.9 amps (because 30 amps ÷ 0.7 = 42.9 amps). According to Table 12.5 on page 191, a #12 is too small, but a #10 is sufficient to carry that much current. However, 19-conductor cable is not available in #10 AWG, and the required maximum rating of the associated overcurrent device is 25 amps, which is not enough to handle the load. Therefore, additional circuits would have to be supplied to properly handle the additional loads.

12.19 If the pins on a stage pin connector become too compressed, they will create a good mechanical and electrical connection with the sockets, which will cause them to heat up and oxidize or arc, resulting in further deterioration of the pins and sockets.

12.20 Yes, it's legal to use a NEMA 5-15P to connect to a NEMA 5-20R.

12.21 A blue CEE 17 rated for 16 amps and 200/250 volts. The voltage in the UK is 240 volts, so, assuming a power factor of 1, the apparent power is 3680 watts.

12.22 *Schuko* is short for the German word *schukokontakt*, meaning "protective contact." The schuko connector is so called because it has earthing clips on the side that make contact with earth before the live conductors make contact, thereby ensuring the device is earthed before it is energized.

References

Beaty HW, Fink DG. *Standard handbook for electrical engineers*. 15th ed. New York: McGraw-Hill; 2007.

British standard BS 7671:2001 — requirements for electrical installations. London: The Institution of Electrical Engineers and BSI; 2004.

Hughes TP. *Networks of power: electrification in Western society, 1880–1930*. Baltimore, Maryland: John Hopkins University Press; 1983.

IAEI soares book on grounding. 8th ed. Richardson, Texas: International Association of Electrical Inspectors; 2001.

Jonnes J. *Empires of light*. New York, New York: Random House; 2004.

McPartland B, McPartland J, Hartwell F. *National Electrical Code® 2008 Handbook*. 26th ed. New York, New York: McGraw Hill; 2008.

Mobsby N. *Practical dimming*. Cambridge, England: Entertainment Technology Press; 2006.

NEC 2008 – NFPA 70: national electrical code. Quincy, Massachusetts: National Fire Protection Association; 2008.

Roberts EW. *Overcurrents and undercurrents: all about GFCIs, AFCIs, and similar devices*. Mystic, Connecticut: Reptec; 2004.

Terry S. New power tools provide quality and efficiency. *Protocol*. Portland, Oregon: Fall 2007.

van Beek M. *Electrical safety for live events*. Cambridge, England: Entertainment Technology Press; 2004.

Index

Page numbers followed by "f" indicate figures and "t" indicate tables

Index